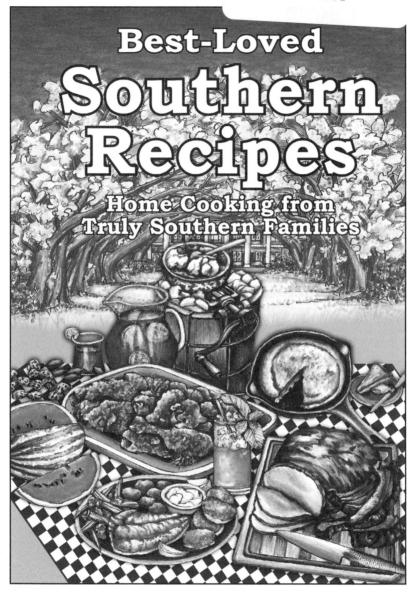

Best-Loved
Southern
Recipes
Home Cooking from
Truly Southern Families

Cookbook Resources, LLC
Highland Village, Texas

Best-Loved Southern Recipes
Home Cooking from Truly Southern Families

Printed September 2011

International Standard Book Number: 978-1-59769-209-0

Library of Congress Control Number: 2011932621

Library of Congress Cataloging-in-Publication Data

> Best-loved Southern recipes : home cooking from truly Southern families.
>   p. cm.
>   Includes bibliographical references and index.
>   ISBN 978-1-931294-51-5
>   1. Cookery, American--Southern style. 2. Cookery--Southern States. I.
> Cookbook Resources, LLC. II. Title.
>   TX715.2.S68B458 2009
>   641.5975--dc22
> 2009010740

Cover and Illustrations by Nancy Bohanan

Edited, Designed and Published in the United States of America
and Manufactured in China by
Cookbook Resources, LLC
541 Doubletree Drive
Highland Village, Texas 75077

Toll free 866-229-2665

www.cookbookresources.com

Bringing Family and Friends to the Table

A Taste of the South

Food and hospitality go hand in hand in the South. From its agricultural beginnings, the South has gained its reputation for good food and good times very honestly. It was common to entertain family and friends surrounded by big tables filled with the best fruits, vegetables and meats the land had to offer.

Historians love to trace the history of foods and dishes of the South because they have such colorful beginnings. During the plantation days, slaves did most of the cooking, and they used seasonings and techniques they brought from Africa. Today, the same seasonings and methods are still used and they continue to preserve the rich cultural mix of the South.

It is easy to describe the South with its food because the agricultural and coastal wealth of the region provides such variety. We incorporated this variety in our cookbook so that the region's personality shines through.

Salted and smoked hams, fried chicken, fried green tomatoes, a mess o' greens, sweet potatoes, pecan pie, barbecue, steamed oysters, soft-shell crabs, sweet tea and grits are easily recognized as belonging to the South.

We collected authentic recipes so you, too, can taste and enjoy some goodness that is unmistakably Southern.

Meet Miss Sadie

Miss Sadie sits on the front porch of her antebellum home and waves at the passers-by. Although she doesn't know everyone in town like she once did, everyone knows her. She was the belle of the ball in her day. Her fried chicken, biscuits and gravy, and fried peach pies were the envy of the town.

Miss Sadie's seen almost as much history as her home. A Southerner through and through, she knows the South. Thanks to some of her well-preserved history, facts and wisdom shared in the pages of this cookbook, we catch a glimpse of the old South.

Contents

Contents

Dedication

With a mission of helping you bring family and friends to the table, Cookbook Resources strives to make family meals and entertaining friends simple, easy and delicious.

We recognize the importance of sharing meals as a means of building family bonds with memories and traditions that will be treasured for a lifetime. Mealtime is an opportunity to sit down with each other and share more than food.

This cookbook is dedicated with gratitude and respect for all those who show their love with homecooked meals, bringing family and friends to the table.

Sunny Appetizers

and

Happy Beverages

Candied Pecans

1 (16 ounce) box light brown sugar
2 teaspoons ground cinnamon
1 teaspoon vanilla
4 cups pecan halves

- Combine brown sugar and cinnamon in medium saucepan and add ½ cup water. Cook until mixture reaches soft-ball stage (234-243°) when dropped into cold water.

- Cook for 15 minutes and add vanilla and pecan halves. Stir until pecans coat well and syrup is thick. Pour immediately onto wax paper and separate halves immediately. Store in airtight container. Yields 4 cups.

Virginia Hot Dip

1 cup chopped pecans
2 teaspoons butter
2 (8 ounce) package cream cheese, softened
¼ cup milk
5 ounces dried beef, minced
1½ teaspoons garlic salt
1 (8 ounce) carton sour cream
2 tablespoons finely minced onion
1 teaspoon hot sauce

- Preheat oven to 350°.

- Saute pecans in butter in skillet and set aside.

- Combine remaining ingredients in bowl and mix thoroughly. Place in sprayed, shallow baking dish and bake for 20 minutes. Remove from oven and sprinkle sauteed pecans over top. Serve hot with crackers or small breadsticks. Yields 1 quart.

Cheesy Pecan Spread

1 (8 ounce) package cream cheese, softened
2 tablespoons milk
1 (2.5 ounce) jar dried beef, shredded
2 tablespoons dried onion flakes
¼ teaspoon garlic powder
¼ cup finely chopped red bell pepper
½ cup sour cream
2 tablespoons butter
½ cup chopped pecans

- Preheat oven to 325°.

- In mixing bowl, combine cream cheese and milk and blend until smooth. Add beef, onion flakes, bell pepper, garlic powder and ¼ teaspoon pepper. Fold in sour cream. Spread mixture in shallow baking dish.

- In saucepan with butter, heat pecans over low heat. Remove from heat, sprinkle over cheese mixture and bake for 30 minutes. Spread on crackers or melba toast rounds. Yields 2 cups.

The fall harvest is the best time to buy pecans in the South.

Fried Cheese Grits Party Bites

1 cup quick-cooking grits
1½ cups shredded extra sharp American cheese
1 egg, slightly beaten
Dash cayenne red pepper
Flour
Shortening

- Cook grits according to package directions. Remove from burner when done and stir in cheese and egg. Continue to stir until cheese melts. Add a dash of cayenne pepper.

- Pour grits into large, shallow dish. Grits should not be more than ½ inch thick in dish. When completely cool, chill for several hours or overnight.

- When ready to serve, slice grits into bite-size pieces. Place in paper bag containing enough flour to coat grits when shaken. Deep fry in hot shortening until golden brown. Drain well and serve immediately. Serves 8.

Grits became the Official State Prepared Food of Georgia in 2002. They are made from bits of ground corn or hominy and are served as a breakfast dish or a side dish.

Peanut Butter Crisps

1 loaf thin-sliced bread
1½ cups vegetable oil
1½ cups peanut butter
Parsley flakes
Crazy salt
Seasoned salt

- Preheat oven to 250°.

- Remove crusts from each slice of bread and cut slices into 4 strips. Place all strips on 1 baking sheet and all crusts and heels on separate baking sheet. Place both baking sheets in oven and bake for 1 hour.

- When toasted, place crusts in blender and make crumbs. Mix oil and peanut butter in bowl until smooth. Mix crumbs with parsley flakes, crazy salt, seasoned salt or any other flavored salt or herb of choice. (Use a light touch with salt so crumbs will not get too salty.)

- Dip strips into oil-peanut butter mixture and roll in crumbs. Dry on wax paper and store in airtight container or freeze. Serves 8.

TIP: *This freezes well so you can make it in advance and enjoy your free time.*

By law, peanut butter must have at least 90% peanuts. If the percentage is less, the product is called peanut spread.

Angels on Horseback

12 slices bacon
1 pint oysters, well drained
Toothpicks
Paprika
Fresh parsley

- Preheat oven to 350°.

- Cut bacon into same number of pieces as oysters and wrap bacon around oysters. Secure with toothpicks.

- Sprinkle each oyster with salt, pepper and paprika. Place on shallow baking pan and bake for 15 to 20 minutes or until brown. Serve on bed of parsley. Serves 6 to 8.

Oyster Tidbits

1 (5 ounce) can smoked oysters, drained, chopped
½ cup herb-seasoned stuffing mix
8 slices bacon, halved, partially cooked

- Preheat oven to 350°.

- In bowl, combine oysters, stuffing mix and ¼ cup water. Form into balls, using about 1 heaping tablespoon mixture for each.

- Wrap half slice bacon around each ball and secure with toothpick. Place on rack in shallow baking pan and bake for 25 to 30 minutes. Drain on paper towels. Serves 6 to 8.

Crab Bites

*This recipe is a scrumptious dish. Serve
as hors d'oeuvres or luncheon sandwich.*

1 (7 ounce) can claw crab
1 cup (2 sticks) butter, softened
1 (5 ounce) jar sharp Old English cheese
½ teaspoon garlic salt or seasoned salt
2 tablespoons mayonnaise
2 dashes Worcestershire sauce
6 English muffins, split

- Preheat oven to 400°.

- In bowl, blend crab, butter, cheese, seasoning, mayonnaise
  and Worcestershire sauce into paste. Spread on muffins. Bake
  thawed for 10 to15 minutes or until brown. Serves 6 to 8.

TIP: Each muffin may be cut into 8 bite-size pieces or left whole.

Quickie Clam Dip

1 (8 ounce) package cream cheese, softened
½ cup sour cream
4 green onions with tops, chopped
2 tablespoons ketchup
1 teaspoon Worcestershire sauce
1 teaspoon seasoned salt
1 (6 ounce) can minced clams

- Combine all ingredients except clams in bowl. Drain clams,
  but do not wash. Mix clams into cream cheese mixture.
  Serves 6.

Southerner's Favorite Crab Dip

2 (8 ounce) packages cream cheese, softened
2 tablespoons milk
1 tablespoon horseradish
2 (6 ounce) cans crabmeat, drained
1 bunch fresh green onions, minced, divided
1 teaspoon garlic salt
⅓ cup slivered almonds, toasted

- Preheat oven to 350°.

- Beat cream cheese, milk and horseradish in bowl. Fold in crabmeat, half green onions and garlic salt.

- Pour mixture into shallow 9 x 9-inch baking dish and top with remaining green onions and almonds. Bake for 20 minutes and serve with wheat crackers. Serves 8 to 10.

Barney's Boiled Peanuts

Usually only true Southerners go for these authentic and traditional boiled peanuts. Yes, boiled.

Raw peanuts

- Pour enough water into large saucepan to cover peanuts. Add a little salt and boil for about 30 minutes. Taste to see if peanuts are done. They should have consistency of cooked dried bean. Add a little more salt, if needed.

- If peanuts are not done, keep boiling and taste every 5 to 10 minutes. Drain peanuts and serve hot or chilled. Store in refrigerator.

Southern Pimiento Cheese

*Everyone has their favorite variation, but this is the basic
pimiento cheese that everyone starts with. If you want to
add minced onions, pickles, jalapenos, cream cheese or
other cheeses, go right ahead and knock yourself out.*

1 (1 pound) package shredded sharp cheddar cheese
3 tablespoons mayonnaise
1 (4 ounce) jar diced pimientos, drained well

- Place cheese in large bowl and add mayonnaise and
  pimientos (make sure pimentos are well drained).
  If you want it drier, don't use as much mayonnaise.
  If you want it creamier, add a little more mayonnaise.
  Serves 4 for sandwiches.

Chicken Liver Bits

½ cup cornmeal
⅓ cup flour
1 teaspoon garlic salt
8 chicken livers, cut into ½ inch pieces
1 egg
2 tablespoons milk
Vegetable oil

- Combine cornmeal, flour, garlic salt and ⅛ teaspoon
  pepper in shallow bowl. Sprinkle livers with additional
  salt and pepper.

- In separate bowl, mix egg and milk.

- Dip each liver piece first into cornmeal mixture, then into
  egg mixture and again into cornmeal mixture. Be sure to
  coat each piece well. Fry liver pieces in deep, hot oil for
  2 minutes or until golden brown. Insert toothpicks and
  serve hot. Serves 4 to 6.

Baked Asparagus Rolls

¾ cup (1½ sticks) butter, softened, divided
½ cup gorgonzola cheese, crumbled
14 slices bread, thin-sliced
1 (15 ounce) can asparagus spears
Grated parmesan cheese

- Preheat oven to 350°.

- In bowl, cream ½ cup butter and gorgonzola cheese. Remove crusts from bread slices and roll each slice flat with rolling pin. Spread cheese mixture on bread.

- Drain asparagus on paper towels. Place 1 spear on bread and roll in jellyroll fashion. Place rolls side by side on baking sheet with seam-side down. Melt remaining butter in saucepan and drizzle over rolls.

- Sprinkle generously with parmesan cheese and bake for 15 to 20 minutes or until crisp and brown. Cut in thirds and serve hot. Serves 8.

TIP: *Make the day before but do not bake. Store in refrigerator. Wait until baking time before sprinkling remaining butter and parmesan cheese.*

Crater of Diamonds State Park is the only active diamond mine in the U.S. and is located near Murfreesboro, Arkansas. It is the world's only diamond mine where the public can prospect for diamonds and keep what they find. The largest find at the site includes the "Uncle Sam", a 40.23-carat stone that is the largest diamond ever found in the U.S. and the "Amarillo Starlight", a 16.37-carat diamond.

Cranberry Punch

This makes a delicious, light pink punch and is wonderful for weddings or parties.

2 (28 ounce) bottles ginger ale
1 (46 ounce) can pineapple juice
1 (1 quart) jar cranberry juice
1 (1 quart) carton pineapple sherbet, softened

- Chill all ingredients. Mix in punch bowl. Serves 30 to 36.

Peach Delight

6 ounces pink lemonade frozen concentrate, thawed
¾ cup vodka
3 - 4 peaches, pitted, peeled
Crushed ice

- Place lemonade, vodka, ¾ cup water and peaches in blender. Mix well. Add crushed ice and blend until smooth. Serves 10 to 12.

Wassail

Double the recipe for a holiday party.

4 (1 quart) jars apple cider
4 (6 ounce) cans lemonade frozen concentrate
1 tablespoon ground cloves
4 sticks cinnamon
½ teaspoon ground allspice

- Heat ingredients in saucepan and boil for 10 to 15 minutes. Serve hot. Serves 32 to 36.

Mary Opal's Reception Punch

4 cups sugar
5 ripe bananas, mashed
Juice of 2 lemons
1 (46 ounce) can pineapple juice
1 (6 ounce) can frozen orange juice concentrate, thawed
2 quarts ginger ale, chilled

- Boil sugar and 6 cups water in saucepan over low heat for 3 minutes. Cool.

- Combine bananas with lemon juice in bowl and add pineapple and orange juice.

- Combine all ingredients except ginger ale in large container and freeze. To serve, thaw for 1 hour 30 minutes, then add ginger ale. Punch will be slushy. Serves 32 to 36.

Fresh Lemonade

14 - 16 lemons
1½ - 2 cups sugar

- Squeeze lemons into large pitcher with 3 quarts cold water. Add sugar and stir well. Serve over cracked ice. Store in refrigerator. Serves 12.

Southerner's Sweet Tea

If you order tea in the South, you'll probably get sweet tea. So if you want hot tea or unsweetened tea, be sure to specify. The real way to make tea is to use actual tea leaves or tea bags. Instant tea, dry concentrate and even canned teas don't qualify for true Southern sweet tea.

4 teaspoons bulk tea
1¼ - 1½ cups sugar
Mint sprigs

• Boil 4 cups water in pot, add tea and remove from heat. Cover and let stand for 10 to 15 minutes.

• Pour 4 cups cold water into pitcher and add sugar. Pour tea through strainer into pitcher and serve over lots of ice. Garnish with sprig of mint. Serves 8.

Summertime Iced Tea

1 cup sugar
6 - 8 small tea bags
6 sprigs fresh mint
½ cup orange juice
¼ cup lemon juice

• Bring 6 cups water to boil in saucepan. Add sugar, tea bags and mint and steep for 5 minutes. Remove tea bags and mint and let cool. Add orange and lemon juices and stir well.

• Chill well before serving. Serves 6.

Instant Spiced Tea Mix

1 (9 ounce) jar Tang®
½ cup instant lemonade mix
1½ cups sugar
1 cup instant tea mix
2 teaspoons ground cinnamon
1 teaspoon ground cloves

• Combine all ingredients in large bowl and mix well. Store in airtight container and shake well before using.

• Use about 2 teaspoons per cup of boiling water. Yields 4 cups.

TIP: Mixture can be stored for about 8 months.

Southern Rum Punch

½ cup pineapple juice
½ cup orange juice
½ cup lime juice
8 dashes Angostura bitters
1 cup (8 ounces) rum
½ cup corn syrup

• Combine ingredients, cover and shake well. Serve in tall glasses over crushed ice. Serves 4 to 6.

The first Kentucky Derby was held in 1875 and has grown in popularity each year since then. More thoroughbred foals come from Kentucky than any other state in the U.S.

Jim Bo's Kentucky Tea

3 tea bags
1¼ cups sugar
1 (6 ounce) can frozen orange juice concentrate
½ (6 ounce) can frozen lemon juice concentrate
¾ cup bourbon
Lemon slices

- Add tea bags to 1½ cups water in saucepan, bring to boil and steep for 5 minutes. Remove tea bags, add 3½ cups water and remaining ingredients and stir until sugar dissolves.

- Place in freezer for about 30 minutes to 1 hour. Scoop slushy drink into tall glasses and garnish with lemon slices. Serves 6 to 8.

Bourbon (or whiskey) originated in Bourbon County, Kentucky. The U.S. government recognized it as uniquely American in 1964 and it is now protected by law.

Good bourbon can be used to replace brandy in most recipes. Bourbon is used in sauces for desserts, main dishes and barbecue.

In the late 1780's, Reverend Elijah Craig, a Baptist minister, developed corn liquor or bourbon whiskey in Scott County, Kentucky. He is one of several to whom the invention is attributed.

Kentucky Mint Julep

Official drink of the Kentucky Derby!

2 cups sugar
¼ cup fresh mint leaves
¼ cup Kentucky bourbon

- Cook 2 cups water and sugar in saucepan over medium-high heat for several minutes and stir constantly. Remove from heat and drop mint leaves in pan. Cover and steam for 30 minutes. Set aside and cool.

- Place cracked ice in glasses and pour in Kentucky bourbon and ½ cup sugar-syrup mixture. Stir well and garnish with mint leaves. Serve with straw. Serves 4.

TIP: Southerners don't like to crush the mint in a julep.

Summertime Brandy Julep

1 teaspoon sugar
12 mint sprigs, divided
½ cup brandy
2 teaspoons light rum
Fresh pineapple slices for garnish

- Dissolve sugar in 1 tablespoon water. Add 6 sprigs of mint and stir vigorously to mix. Add brandy and stir.

- Pack old-fashioned glasses with crushed ice. Pour in brandy mixture and stir. Add rum and stir. Place glasses in freezer for about 30 minutes to frost glasses.

- Decorate with pineapple slices, lime slices or other fresh fruit and remaining mint sprigs. Serves 4.

Warm-Your-Soul Soups

and

Stylish Salads

Ham and Fresh Okra Soup

1 ham hock
1 cup frozen butter beans or lima beans
1½ pounds cooked, cubed ham or chicken
1 (15 ounce) can chopped stewed tomatoes
3 cups small whole okra
2 large onions, diced
Rice, cooked

- Boil ham hock in 1½ quarts water in soup pot for about
  1 hour 30 minutes. Add remaining ingredients and slow boil
  for additional 1 hour. Season with a little salt and pepper
  and serve over rice. Serves 6 to 8.

Quick and Easy Peanut Soup

¼ cup (½ stick) butter
1 onion, finely chopped
2 ribs celery, chopped
2 (10 ounce) cans cream of chicken soup
2 soup cans milk
1¼ cups crunchy peanut butter

- Melt butter in saucepan and saute onion and celery over low
  heat. Blend in soup and milk and stir. Add peanut butter
  and continue to heat until mixture blends well. Serves 4 to 6.

Slow-Cook Navy Bean and Ham Soup

Better than Grandma's!

1½ cups dry navy beans
1 carrot, finely chopped
¼ cup finely chopped celery
1 small onion, finely chopped
1 (¾ pound) ham hock

- Soak beans for 8 to 12 hours and drain. Place all ingredients, 5 cups water, ½ teaspoon salt and a little pepper in 2-quart slow cooker. Cook for 8 to 10 hours on LOW setting.

- Remove ham hock and discard skin, fat and bone. Cut meat in small pieces and place in soup. Beans can be mashed, if desired. Serves 6 to 8.

Miss Sadie: *"Southerners love a good pot o' beans. You can't beat black-eyed peas, butter beans or limas seasoned just right. If you ask a Southerner about a pot o' beans, you'll get an earful, that's for sure."*

Edna Earle's Cold Peach Soup

This is delicious for summer luncheons with
vegetables or chicken salad sandwiches.

2 pounds peaches
1 tablespoon lemon juice
3 tablespoons quick-cooking tapioca
3 tablespoons sugar
1 (6 ounce) can frozen orange juice concentrate

- Puree peaches with lemon juice in blender and set aside.

- Combine tapioca, sugar, a little salt and 1 cup water in
  saucepan. Heat to full boil and stir constantly.

- Transfer to medium-sized bowl. Stir in orange juice until
  it melts. Add 1½ cups water and stir until smooth. Mix in
  pureed peaches, cover and chill. Serve cold. Serves 8.

TIP: Make this soup before you need it so it has time to chill.

Georgia is ranked 3rd in production of
peaches with most being harvested between May
and August.

Carolina She-Crab Soup

4 cups milk
¼ teaspoon mace
1 teaspoon grated lemon peel
1 pound crabmeat, flaked
2 (1 pint) cartons whipping cream
¼ cup (½ stick) butter
½ cup cracker crumbs
2 tablespoons sherry

- Combine milk, mace and lemon peel in double boiler and simmer for 5 minutes. Add crabmeat, cream and butter and cook over low heat for 15 minutes.

- Stir in cracker crumbs a little at a time to get consistency desired and season soup with a little salt and pepper. Cover, remove from heat and set aside for 5 to 10 minutes so flavors blend. Add sherry before serving. Serves 6 to 8.

Something like a bisque, something like a chowder, she crab soup has been a traditional dish with origins dating back to the early 1700's in the Charleston, South Carolina area.

__Miss Sadie:__ "If you die before you get to the Low Country to eat some she crab soup, then you better make it to heaven 'cause they serve it ever' day there."

Everybody's Seafood Gumbo

¼ cup (½ stick) butter
¼ cup flour
1½ - 2 pounds okra, sliced
6 firm tomatoes
½ cup minced onion
2 pounds shrimp
1 pound crabmeat
1 pound fish filets
Cayenne pepper
1 pint fresh oysters with liquor

- Melt butter in heavy skillet and add flour. Stir well over medium heat to make smooth, paste-like roux. Add 2 quarts water, okra, tomatoes and onion and cook on low for 45 minutes.

- Wash, clean and peel shrimp. Flake crabmeat and remove any pieces of shell. Remove all bones and skin from fish.

- When roux is rich brown color, add a little salt, pepper and cayenne pepper and mix well. Add all seafood and cook on medium-low heat for 30 minutes or until desired consistency. Serve over rice. Serves 6 to 8.

"Beaufort Town" was a seaport established in 1722. It had the right to collect customs. It was also called "Fish Town" in the 1700's after Blackbeard frequented the coast.

Pirate Stew

If you can open cans, you can make this stew. Don't let the number of ingredients get to you. Leave something out if you get tired of opening cans. Of course, you can make this from scratch; it will just take more time.

3 pounds chuck steak, cubed
Canola oil
2 (15 ounce) cans diced tomatoes
4 (16 ounce) cans cocktail vegetable juice
1 (28 ounce) can green beans
2 (15 ounce) cans field peas with snaps
2 (15 ounce) cans sliced squash
2 (15 ounce) cans green peas
2 (14 ounce) cans cut okra
2 (16 ounce) packages frozen lima beans
3 (16 ounce) packages frozen cut yellow corn
1 (16 ounce) package frozen white corn
3 pounds onion, peeled, diced
4 pounds potatoes, cubed
Seasoned salt
Rosemary
Bay leaf
Curry powder
Thyme

- Brown steak in oil in soup pot. Add 1 quart water and vegetables and season with pepper and remaining ingredients. Simmer all day. Remove excess fat
  Serves 8 to 12.

TIP: This recipe makes enough for several meals so freeze some for later.

Wild Rabbit Stew

1 dressed rabbit, cut up
½ cup (1 stick) butter
2 garlic cloves, minced
1 medium onion, sliced
½ cup vegetable oil
1 (8 ounce) can tomato juice
¼ cup white vinegar
¼ cup green olives, sliced
10 drops hot sauce
5 medium potatoes, peeled, sliced
1 cup sherry

- Brown rabbit in butter in large heavy skillet. Add garlic, onion, oil, tomato juice, vinegar, olives, hot sauce and ½ teaspoon salt. Bring mixture to a boil, reduce heat and simmer for 1 hour.

- Add potatoes and sherry and continue to cook for additional 20 minutes or until potatoes are tender. Serves 4 to 6.

Miss Sadie: *"Huntin' is just a fact of life around here and Southerners eat what they kill. If it has wings, we fry it. If it swims, we fry it. And if it's tough, we just cook it real slow."*

Sister's Brunswick Stew

*This signature southern dish takes longer than most dishes,
but it is so worth it. Cook meat one day and put stew
together the next day. You'll have enough to freeze and serve
for several meals. It makes an excellent one-dish meal.*

1 (4 pound) boneless pork loin
4 - 6 chicken fryers or 6 pounds boneless, skinless
     chicken pieces
9 medium potatoes, quartered
6 (28 ounce) cans stewed diced tomatoes
2 teaspoons sugar
½ medium onion, chopped
3 (16 ounce) packages frozen butter beans, thawed
4 (16 ounce) packages frozen sweet corn, thawed

- Cut pork and chicken into bite-size pieces. Cover with water
  in large saucepan and cook very slowly until firm. Remove
  any bones and skin. Skim off excess fat.

- Return meat to broth, add potatoes and cook on medium.
  When done, mash potatoes to thicken broth. Add tomatoes,
  sugar, a little salt and pepper and cook until soupy. Add
  onion and butter beans. Cook on low and stir frequently.

- Add corn last because it may stick to bottom of pan. Cook
  over low heat until butter beans and corn are done. (Keep
  scraping bottom of pan to prevent sticking.) Serves 18 to 20.

Miss Sadie: *"There are lots of variations on this
recipe. Ever'body's gonna give you their opinion
for sure."*

Frogmore Stew

*Frogmore Stew originates in South Carolina's Low Country and
dates back many years. According to one story passed down
through the years, an old fisherman gathered up whatever he
could find to put in a stew. Other stories credit specific people on
St. Helena Island with the invention, but there's no disagreement
to the fact that Frogmore Stew is a combination of sausage,
seafood and corn. Here's one version of the famous dish.*

¼ cup Old Bay seafood seasoning
3 pounds smoked link sausage, sliced
3 onions, peeled, chopped
1 lemon, sliced, seeded
½ cup (1 stick) butter
6 ears corn, broken in half
3 pounds large shrimp with peel
Cocktail sauce

- Add about 2 gallons water, Old Bay seasoning, sausage,
  onions, lemon, salt and pepper in large stew pot. Bring
  to a boil. Simmer for 45 minutes.

- Add butter and corn and cook for 10 minutes. Add shrimp
  and cook for additional 5 minutes. Drain. Remove with
  slotted spoon to serving platter. Serve with cocktail sauce.
  Serves 8 to 12.

Miss Sadie: *"Yes, well, you're gonna get a bunch
of opinions on this recipe. Southerners all have their
favorite way o' doin' things, you know."*

Clam Chowder

This is so good you may want to double it.

3 large potatoes
2 medium onions
3 slices bacon
1 pound fresh clams or 2 (6 ounce) cans minced clams
1 bottle clam juice
1 tablespoon Worcestershire sauce
2 tablespoons cornmeal

- Dice potatoes and onions, place in pot with enough water to cover and cook until soft. While potatoes cook, fry bacon crisp enough to crumble. Save bacon drippings and add to potato mixture along with crumbled bacon. Simmer mixture for 1 minute.

- Add clams, clam juice, salt, pepper and Worcestershire sauce. Thicken with cornmeal, but stir constantly so it will not be lumpy. Serve for lunch or as preface to full meal. Serves 6 to 8.

TIP: Serve this immediately. It won't freeze.

Marinated Cucumbers

1 cup vinegar
½ cup sugar
1 tablespoon chives
6 cucumbers, peeled

- Combine vinegar, sugar, chives and ½ teaspoon salt in large measuring cup. Slice cucumbers about ⅓ inch thick and place in large bowl. Pour marinade over cucumbers, cover and chill. Serves 8.

Carrot Salad Supreme

2 (3 ounce) packages lemon gelatin
1 tablespoon vinegar or lemon juice
1 (20 ounce) can crushed pineapple with juice
1 cup shredded sharp cheddar cheese
1 cup grated carrots
¾ cup chopped pecans

- Dissolve gelatin in 2 cups boiling water in bowl and add vinegar and ½ teaspoon salt. Chill slightly. Drain pineapple and add enough water to juice to equal 2 cups.

- Fold in cheese, carrots, pineapple, juice and water, and pecans. Pour into mold rinsed in cold water and chill until firm. Unmold on platter and serve plain or use dressing consisting of 2 parts mayonnaise and 1 part sour cream. Serves 8.

Fresh Okra Salad

Fresh okra
Vinaigrette salad dressing

- Wash okra and cut off ends. Add okra to saucepan with boiling, salted water. Cook just until almost tender. Drain and toss with your favorite salad dressing.

Traditional Coleslaw

½ cup sugar
½ cup vinegar
¼ cup milk
1 - 2 cups mayonnaise
1 large head cabbage
1 - 2 carrots, grated, optional

- Combine sugar, vinegar, milk and just enough mayonnaise to make dressing consistency in bowl. Add salt and pepper to taste.

- Discard outside leaves of cabbage, wash remaining leaves and chop finely in food processor or on grater. Grate carrots and mix with cabbage. Mix dressing and cabbage well, cover and chill. Serves 8 to 10.

Spinach Salad Mold

1 (10 ounce) package frozen chopped spinach, thawed
1 (3 ounce) package lemon or lime gelatin
1 cup mayonnaise
1 cup cottage cheese, drained
⅓ cup diced celery
⅓ cup diced onion

- Squeeze liquid from thawed spinach and set aside. Do not cook.

- Dissolve gelatin in ¾ cup boiling water in bowl and set aside to cool.

- Combine spinach and remaining ingredients with gelatin and mix well. Pour mixture into ring mold and chill until firm. Unmold and garnish as desired to serve. Serves 8.

Williamsburg Salad

2 (1 ounce) packets unflavored gelatin
½ cup vinegar
1 cup sugar
1 cup chopped pecans
1 cup sweet pickle relish
1 cup crushed pineapple, drained, set aside ½ cup juice
1 cup sliced stuffed olives

- Soften gelatin in ½ cup water and dissolve in 1 cup boiling water in bowl. Add vinegar, ½ teaspoon salt, sugar, pecans, relish, pineapple, pineapple juice and olives. Pour into molds and chill. Serves 8 to 10.

Savory Layer Salad

Make this salad the day before you need it.

2½ cups mayonnaise
1 (16 ounce) carton sour cream
1 teaspoon Worcestershire sauce
Hot sauce
¼ cup lemon juice
1 package fresh spinach, torn in pieces
1 head iceberg lettuce, torn in pieces
1 cup (or less) sliced green onions
1 pound bacon, cooked, crumbled
6 eggs, hard-boiled, sliced
1 (10 ounce) package frozen green peas, thawed
1½ cups shredded Swiss cheese

- Combine mayonnaise, sour cream, Worcestershire sauce, dash of hot sauce, lemon juice, and a little salt and pepper in bowl and mix well.

- Combine salad greens, onion and crumbled bacon.

- Pour salad mixture into 9 x 13-inch baking dish and spread mayonnaise mixture evenly over salad. Layer eggs and peas. Top with Swiss cheese. Cover and chill for 24 hours. Serves 12 to 16.

The Mason-Dixon Line is the boundary between Pennsylvania and Maryland surveyed in the 1760's by Charles Mason and Jeremiah Dixon to settle a border dispute between the colonies. It separates portions of Pennsylvania, Delaware, Maryland and what is now West Virginia. Over time it has come to mean the division of the North and the South.

Perfect Potato Salad

3 medium potatoes
1 teaspoon sugar
1 teaspoon vinegar
½ cup sliced celery
⅓ cup finely chopped onion
¼ cup sweet pickle relish
1 teaspoon celery seed
¾ cup mayonnaise or salad dressing
2 eggs, hard-boiled, sliced

- Cook whole potatoes in enough boiling salted water to cover for 25 minutes or until tender. Drain well and peel. Cut potatoes in quarters and slice ¼ inch thick.

- Add 1 teaspoon salt and remaining ingredients except mayonnaise and eggs. Stir mixture. Fold in mayonnaise; then carefully fold in egg slices. Cover and chill. Serves 8.

> Rice came to the South by way of a storm-ravaged merchant ship sailing from Madagascar and reaching the port of Charleston for safe haven. As a gift to the people, the ship's captain gave a local planter "Golden Seed Rice" and by 1700, rice was a major crop in the colonies. The success of the crop gave rise to the name "Carolina Gold Rice".

Rice Salad

2 (6 ounce) packages chicken Rice-a-Roni®
¾ cup chopped green bell pepper
8 green onions, chopped
16 stuffed or ripe olives, sliced
2 (6 ounce) jars marinated artichoke hearts, drained,
     chopped, set aside liquid
½ - ⅔ cup mayonnaise
½ teaspoon curry powder, optional

- Cook rice according to package directions in saucepan, but omit butter. Cool.

- Add bell pepper, green onions, olives and drained artichokes.

- In separate bowl, mix liquid from artichokes with mayonnaise and curry powder. Add to rice mixture and press into mold. Chill. Serves 8 to 12.

Chilled Cranberry Salad

1 (8 ounce) package cream cheese, softened
½ cup powdered sugar
1 tablespoon lemon juice
½ cup mayonnaise
1 (16 ounce) can whole cranberry sauce
1 cup whipped topping, thawed

- Beat cream cheese, powdered sugar, lemon juice and mayonnaise in bowl and blend well. Add cranberry sauce and whipped topping to cream cheese mixture and turn into 8 x 8-inch pan. Chill. Cut into squares before serving. Serves 9.

Dreamy Blueberry Salad

1 (8 ounce) can crushed pineapple with juice
2 (3 ounce) packages raspberry gelatin
1 (16 ounce) can blueberries, drained

- Drain pineapple and add enough water to pineapple juice to make 2 cups. Pour into saucepan and bring to a boil. Pour hot liquid over gelatin and dissolve.

- Chill until mixture is consistency of egg whites. Mix blueberries and pineapple into gelatin, pour into a 9 x 9-inch pan and chill until it congeals.

Topping:

1 (8 ounce) package cream cheese
1 (8 ounce) carton sour cream
½ cup sugar
½ cup chopped pecans

- Beat cream cheese, sour cream and sugar in bowl. Stir in pecans. Spread over congealed salad. Serves 9.

Strawberry Salad

2 (3 ounce) packages strawberry gelatin
2 (10 ounce) packages frozen strawberries, thawed
1 cup crushed pineapple with juice
1 cup chopped walnuts
2 bananas, sliced
1 (16 ounce) carton sour cream

- Dissolve gelatin in 1⅔ cups boiling water in saucepan. Add frozen strawberries, remove from heat and stir occasionally until strawberries thaw.

- Add crushed pineapple, nuts and bananas. Pour half mixture into 9 x 9-inch pan and chill for 1 hour 30 minutes or until firm. Spread sour cream over firm mixture and pour remaining mixture over top. Chill until set. Serves 12.

TIP: If you desire, substitute pecans for walnuts.

A native wild strawberry grown on the eastern coast called Fragaria Virginiana was the start of today's strawberries, now grown primarily in California. Cultivation of the wild Virginia strawberry started sometime in the 1630's by colonists who learned about the fruit from Native Americans.

St. Pat's Pear Salad

1 (10 ounce) jar mint jelly
1 (20 ounce) can pear halves, with liquid
Green food coloring
Bibb lettuce
Salad dressing
Mint leaves

- Combine mint jelly and ½ cup pear liquid in saucepan over low heat. Add drops of green food coloring.

- Place 8 pear halves in melted jelly and set aside. Baste occasionally until pears turn light green in color. Drain pears.

- Arrange two pear halves with cut-side up on individual salad plates over lettuce. Fill pears with spoonful favorite salad dressing and garnish with mint leaves. Serves 4.

Thanksgiving's Berry Salad

A grand accompaniment with turkey or chicken salad!

1 (1 ounce) packet unflavored gelatin
1 (6 ounce) package raspberry or cherry gelatin
1 (15 ounce) can crushed pineapple with juice
1 (14 ounce) jar cranberry-orange relish
1 cup chopped pecans

- Dissolve unflavored gelatin in ¼ cup cold water in bowl.

- In separate bowl, dissolve flavored gelatin in 1¼ cups boiling water. Mix remaining ingredients and gelatin mixture and pour into 9 x 13-inch pan or 2-quart mold. Chill until set. Serves 8 to 10.

Chicken Salad Surprise

*Delicious recipe with sliced fresh fruit such as apples
and bananas or natural cheddar or Havarti cheese.*

2½ cups cooked, diced chicken
½ cup diced celery
½ cup diced apple with peel
½ cup blanched, slivered almonds, toasted
1 small onion, minced
⅓ cup mayonnaise
1 teaspoon lemon juice
1 - 2 teaspoons curry powder
Lettuce leaves

- Combine chicken, celery, apple, almonds and onion in bowl.

- In separate bowl, combine mayonnaise with lemon juice,
  ½ teaspoon salt, ⅛ teaspoon pepper and curry powder. Stir
  into chicken mixture. Serve on crisp lettuce leaves or as a
  sandwich. Serves 6 to 8.

*Alabama is the home of the U.S. Space Camp and
the U.S. Space and Rocket Center.*

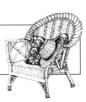

*Alabama workers built the first rocket to place
humans on the moon.*

Congealed Chicken Salad

This recipe is a great luncheon dish with
asparagus and baby beets or pickled peaches.
It can be made several days before you need it.

2 (1 ounce) packets unflavored gelatin
1½ cups chicken broth
1 cup finely diced celery
1 small finely diced onion
1 (8 ounce) can baby green peas, drained
½ cup chopped nuts
3 cups cooked, diced chicken
4 eggs, hard-boiled, chopped
3 tablespoons sweet pickle relish
1 (2 ounce) jar chopped pimientos
1 cup mayonnaise

• Dissolve gelatin in ½ cup cold water in bowl and pour in hot chicken broth. Add remaining ingredients. Place mixture in flat casserole or in 15 individual molds. Chill. Serves 15.

Alabama	Residents are called Alabamians or Alabamans.
Arkansas	Residents are called Arkansans.
Georgia	Residents are called Georgians.
Kentucky	Residents are called Kentuckians.
Maryland	Residents are called Marylanders.

Hot Chicken Salad

4 cups cooked, diced cold chicken
2 cups chopped celery
4 eggs, hard-boiled, diced
2 tablespoons finely minced onions
2 tablespoons lemon juice
¾ cup mayonnaise
¾ cup cream of chicken soup
1 cup shredded cheese
1½ cups crushed potato chips
⅔ cup toasted, finely chopped almonds

- Combine chicken, celery, eggs, onion, 1 teaspoon salt, lemon juice, mayonnaise and soup in bowl and mix well. Pour into 9 x 13-inch baking dish.

- In separate bowl, combine cheese, potato chips and almonds and spread over top. Cover and chill overnight.

- When ready to bake, preheat oven to 400°.

- Bake for 20 to 25 minutes. Serves 8.

Mississippi	*Residents are called Mississippians.*
North Carolina	*Residents are called North Carolinians.*
South Carolina	*Residents are called South Carolinians.*
Tennessee	*Residents are called Tennesseans.*
Virginia	*Residents are called Virginians.*
West Virginia	*Residents are called West Virginians.*

Shrimp Salad Mold

2 (1 ounce) packets unflavored gelatin
1 (10 ounce) can tomato soup, heated
¼ cup chopped onion
¼ cup chopped green bell pepper
1 tablespoon lemon juice
1 (8 ounce) package cream cheese, softened
1 cup mayonnaise
1 cup chopped celery
2 cups cooked, shelled, veined, bite-size shrimp

• Dissolve gelatin in ¼ cup cold water in bowl and add to heated soup.

• Puree onion, bell pepper, lemon juice and ¼ teaspoon salt in blender and add to soup mixture.

• Beat cream cheese and mayonnaise in bowl until smooth. Add to soup mixture. Stir in celery and shrimp. Pour into 9-inch mold and chill. Serves 9.

Washington, Arkansas was founded in 1824 and was a popular stop for travelers headed for Texas on the Southwest Trail. Sam Houston, Davy Crockett and Jim Bowie traveled through Washington on their way to Texas. A local blacksmith, James Black, is said to have crafted the legendary Bowie knife for Jim Bowie in his shop in Washington.

Butter-Melting Breads

Prize Pickles and Preserves

Angel Biscuits

3 packages yeast
5 cups flour
⅓ cup sugar
1 cup shortening
2 cups buttermilk*

- Dissolve yeast in ⅓ cup warm water in bowl and set aside.

- In separate bowl, combine flour and sugar and cut in shortening. Add buttermilk and yeast and stir. Chill. Dough should last about 10 days in plastic container in refrigerator.

- On floured board or wax paper, pat out enough dough for the meal. Cut out biscuits and place on sprayed baking pan. Let rise in warm place for 2 to 3 hours.

- When ready to bake, preheat oven to 425°.

- Bake for 12 minutes or until brown.

*TIP: To make buttermilk, mix 1 cup milk with 1 tablespoon lemon juice or vinegar and let milk stand for about 10 minutes.

Luncheon Muffins

1 cup (2 sticks) butter, softened
2 cups flour
1 (8 ounce) carton sour cream

- Preheat oven to 350°.

- Combine all ingredients in bowl and mix well. Pour mixture into sprayed muffin cups and bake for 20 to 25 minutes. Serves 8.

Rich Dinner Rolls

1 cup milk
¼ cup sugar
¼ cup (½ stick) butter, softened
2 packages yeast or yeast cakes
2 eggs, beaten
5¼ cups flour, divided
Melted butter

- Scald milk in saucepan over low heat. Stir in sugar, 1 teaspoon salt and butter. Remove from heat and cool to lukewarm. Pour ½ cup warm water into large warm bowl, sprinkle or crumble in yeast and stir until it dissolves. Add lukewarm milk mixture, eggs and 2 cups flour. Beat until smooth.

- Stir in enough remaining flour to make soft dough and turn out onto lightly floured board. Knead for 8 to 10 minutes or until smooth and elastic. Place in greased bowl and turn to grease top. Cover and let rise in warm place (free from draft) for 30 minutes or until doubled in bulk.

- Punch down and divide dough into 3 equal pieces. Form each piece into 9-inch roll. Cut into 9 equal pieces and form into smooth balls. Place in 3 sprayed round cake pans. Cover and let rise for 30 minutes or until doubled in bulk.

- When ready to bake, preheat oven to 375°.

- Brush lightly with melted butter and bake for 15 to 20 minutes. Yields 27 rolls.

The Georgia State Capitol, under construction from 1883 to 1889, was dedicated as a National Historic Landmark in 1977.

Buttermilk Refrigerator Rolls

3 packages dry yeast
5 cups flour
¼ cup sugar
¾ cup shortening, melted
2 cups buttermilk*

- Dissolve yeast in ¼ cup warm water in bowl and set aside.

- In separate bowl, combine flour, sugar and shortening. Add buttermilk and yeast mixture and mix thoroughly by hand. Add more flour, if needed. Cover and chill. Use dough as needed.

- About 1 hour 30 minutes before baking, shape dough pieces into 1-inch balls and place in muffin cups, three to a cup. Prepare as many rolls as needed and chill remaining dough.

- Cover rolls and let rise in warm place for 1 hour before baking.

- When ready to bake, preheat oven to 425°.

- Bake for 12 minutes or until brown. Dough will last 10 days in plastic container in refrigerator. Yields 24 to 30 rolls.

*TIP: To make buttermilk, mix 1 cup milk with 1 tablespoon lemon juice or vinegar and let milk stand for about 10 minutes.

Miss Sadie: *"Honey, if you don't keep buttermilk in your ice box, just get out 1 cup of milk and put 1 tablespoon of lemon juice or vinegar in there. Leave it alone for 10 minutes and you've got buttermilk. But honey, have you ever tried a big ol' glass of cold buttermilk? Mmm, mmm!"*

Banana-Nut Bread

½ cup (1 stick) butter
1 cup sugar
2 eggs
2 cups flour
1 teaspoon baking soda
1 teaspoon ground cinnamon
4 ripe bananas
1 cup chopped pecans

- Preheat oven to 350°.

- Cream butter and sugar in bowl and add eggs one at a time. Stir vigorously.

- In separate bowl, combine flour, baking soda and cinnamon and stir into butter mixture a little at a time. Mash bananas and add to mixture. Stir well and add pecans.

- Pour into sprayed loaf pan and bake for 50 to 60 minutes. Serves 6.

The Low Country refers to the coastal counties of South Carolina, especially the area of Charleston and south of Charleston, including the Sea Islands. The term is also used more generally for all the counties below the fall line in South Carolina.

"No Need to Knead" Rolls

2 packages dry yeast
1 egg
¼ cup shortening
6½ cups flour

- Combine 2 cups lukewarm water, 1½ teaspoons salt and remaining ingredients in bowl, mix well and shape into rolls. Place rolls in sprayed round cake pans.

- Cover and let rise for 1 hour 30 minutes to 2 hours.

- When ready to bake, preheat oven to 400°.

- Bake for 15 to 20 minutes. Yields 30.

Indians lived in Kentucky as much as 13,000 years ago. When European settlers came to the territory, they brought diseases that almost wiped out the native population.

In the 1750's and 1760's, settlers came to the territory after hearing stories of enough game and land for everyone. The first permanent settlements were established in the 1770's and one, established by Daniel Boone, was called Fort Boonesborough.

Christmas Cranberry Bread

2 cups flour
1 cup sugar
1½ teaspoons baking powder
½ teaspoon baking soda
¼ cup shortening
¾ cup orange juice
1 tablespoon grated orange peel
1 egg, well beaten
½ cup chopped nuts
1 (16 ounce) can whole cranberry sauce

- Preheat oven to 350°.

- Sift flour, sugar, baking powder, baking soda and 1 teaspoon salt in bowl. Cut in shortening until mixture resembles coarse cornmeal.

- In separate bowl, combine orange juice, orange peel and egg and pour into dry ingredients. Mix just enough to dampen and fold in nuts and cranberry sauce. Spoon mixture into sprayed loaf pan and spread corners and sides slightly higher than center.

- Bake for 1 hour until crust is brown and center is done. Remove, cool and store overnight for easy slicing. Serves 6 to 8.

Zucchini Bread

3 eggs
2 cups sugar
1 cup vegetable oil
2 cups grated zucchini with peel
3 cups flour
1 teaspoon ground cinnamon
1 teaspoon baking powder
1 teaspoon baking soda
1 cup chopped nuts
1 teaspoon vanilla

- Preheat oven to 350°.

- Mix all ingredients and 1 teaspoon salt in bowl and pour into 2 sprayed loaf pans. Bake for 1 hour or until golden brown. Serves 8 to 12.

Cumberland Falls State Park in the Daniel Boone National Forest in Kentucky is called the "Niagara of the South". The waterfall spans more than 125 feet across and water falls more than 60 feet to the gorge below. On clear nights with a full moon, a phenomenon known as a moonbow can be seen through the mist of the water. Cumberland Falls is believed to have the most predictable moonbow in the world because it occurs every full moon when the sky is clear and the waterfall is misty enough.

Pumpkin Bread

3⅓ cups flour
2 teaspoons baking soda
1 teaspoon ground cinnamon
1 teaspoon ground nutmeg
4 eggs
2 cups cooked pumpkin
1 cup vegetable oil
3 cups sugar
1 cup nuts

- Preheat oven to 350°.

- Combine flour, baking soda, 1½ teaspoons salt, cinnamon and nutmeg in bowl and mix well. Add ⅔ cup water and remaining ingredients to mixture and mix well.

- Pour mixture into 2 sprayed loaf pans about three-fourths full and bake for 45 minutes or until toothpick inserted in center comes out clean. Serves 8 to 12.

TIP: Add 1 cup raisins and ¼ cup shredded coconut to above recipe.

Mammoth Cave National Park in south central Kentucky is the longest known cave system in the world. The park contains more than 52,000 acres and is home to more than 900 varieties of flowers, 21 of which are endangered or threatened.

Williamsburg Sally Lunn Bread

1 package yeast or yeast cake
1 cup warm milk
½ cup (1 stick) butter
⅓ cup sugar
3 eggs, beaten
4 cups flour

- Put yeast in warm milk.

- Cream butter, sugar and eggs in bowl. Add yeast-milk mixture. Sift flour into mixture and mix well. Let rise in warm place.

- Punch down and place into sprayed mold or 3-quart ring mold. Let rise again.

- When ready to bake, preheat oven to 350°.

- Bake for 45 minutes or until done. Serve hot. Serves 6 to 8.

The first representative assembly in the American colonies was founded in Virginia in 1619.

Southern Spoon Bread

3 eggs
3 cups milk
1 cup white cornmeal
1 teaspoon butter, melted
1 teaspoon sugar

- Preheat oven to 350°.

- Separate eggs and beat yolks in bowl.

- In separate bowl, beat egg whites until stiff. Set aside.

- Scald milk in double boiler, add cornmeal gradually and cook for 5 minutes. Stir until very smooth. Cool slightly and add butter, sugar and 1 teaspoon salt.

- Add egg yolks and fold in egg whites. Pour into sprayed 9 x 9-inch baking dish and bake for 45 minutes. Serves 9.

Many southern writers including Eudora Welty, Tennessee Williams, William Faulkner, Katherine Anne Porter, Flannery O'Connor, Thomas Wolfe and Robert Penn Warren expertly represent American literature of the 20th century.

Virginia Spoon Bread

1 cup cornmeal
1 tablespoon sugar
¼ cup (½ stick) butter
3 eggs
2 teaspoons baking powder
1⅓ cups milk

- Preheat oven to 350°.

- Combine cornmeal, sugar and 1 teaspoon salt in bowl. Add 1⅓ cups boiling water and butter to mixture. Stir constantly and set aside to cool.

- In separate bowl, beat eggs until light. Stir eggs, baking powder and milk into batter and mix well.

- Pour into sprayed 2-quart baking dish and place dish in baking pan with about ½ inch water. Bake for about 30 to 35 minutes or until set. Serves 8 to 10.

The name "Virginia" was given in honor of Elizabeth I, the virgin queen of England.

Miss Sadie: "Oh my, I'll never forget going to Colonial Williamsburg and eatin' at Christina Campbell's Tavern. Their spoon bread was just wonderful! You know George Washington ate there. Well, not when I was there, of course."

Sourdough Starter and Bread

Starter:

1 package yeast
2 cups flour

- Use only glass bowl for mixing and do NOT leave metal utensils in starter. Dissolve yeast in 2 cups warm water in glass bowl. Add flour and mix well. Place starter in warm place overnight. Next morning, cover container and chill. Use only glass container to store starter. Chill and cover starter when not in use.

Every 5 days stir into starter:

1 cup milk
¼ cup sugar
1 cup flour

- Do not use starter on day it is "fed". Always keep at least 2 cups mixture in container. Starter may be fed more frequently than every 5 days.

Sourdough Bread:

2 cups flour
1 tablespoon baking powder
2 tablespoons sugar
1 egg
2 cups Sour Dough Starter

- Combine flour, baking powder, sugar and 1 teaspoon salt in bowl. Add egg and starter and mix well. Pour into greased loaf pan. Place in warm place and allow to double in bulk.

- When ready to bake, preheat oven to 350°.

- Bake for 30 to 35 minutes. Serves 8 to 10.

Cook's Best Cornbread

*This is moist, much like spoon bread. It's also
very good reheated and great with maple syrup.*

2 eggs
1 (8 ounce) carton sour cream
½ cup vegetable oil
1 (8 ounce) can cream-style corn
1 cup cornmeal
3 teaspoons baking powder

- Preheat oven to 375°.

- Beat eggs, sour cream, oil and corn in bowl. Blend in
  cornmeal, baking powder and 1½ teaspoons salt.

- Pour in sprayed 9 x 9-inch pan. Bake for 30 to 50 minutes.
  Serves 6 to 9.

Cornmeal Pone

2 cups cornmeal
¼ cup vegetable oil

- Combine cornmeal, 2 cups cold water and 1 teaspoon salt in
  bowl and stir well. Set aside for 2 minutes.

- Heat oil in flat-bottomed skillet. Drop tablespoonfuls of
  mixture into hot oil and fry until brown on both sides. Serve
  with ham slices or vegetable meal. Serves 4 to 6.

Eastern North Carolina Cornbread

1 cup cornmeal
½ cup flour
2 teaspoons baking powder
2 teaspoons sugar
1 cup milk
2 eggs
½ cup shortening, melted

- Preheat oven to 400°.

- Sift cornmeal, flour, baking powder, 1 teaspoon salt and sugar into bowl. Stir in milk and add eggs, one at a time. Add shortening.

- Pour into sprayed baking pan or muffin cups and bake for 20 to 25 minutes. Serves 6.

Virginia Dare was the first child born to British settlers in America in 1587 at Roanoke, North Carolina. Her birth is commemorated in "The Lost Colony" outdoor drama presented annually in Albemarle since 1937.

Miss Sadie: *"In the South you better know how to make good cornbread. Bad cornbread is against the law."*

Cornbread Muffins or Squares

1¼ cups cornmeal
¾ cup flour
3 teaspoons baking powder
1 egg
⅓ cup vegetable oil
⅔ cup milk

- Preheat oven to 400°.

- Combine cornmeal, flour, baking powder and 1 teaspoon salt in bowl.

- In separate bowl, combine egg, oil and milk. Combine liquid and dry ingredients and mix well with spoon.

- Fill 12 sprayed muffin cups two-thirds full and bake for 25 minutes. For squares, pour into sprayed 7 x 11-inch pan. Serves 6.

Golden-Fried Hush Puppies

1 cup flour
¾ cup cornmeal
1 cup finely minced onion
1¼ teaspoons baking powder
Milk
Vegetable oil

- Combine flour, cornmeal, onion, baking powder and a little salt in bowl. Add just enough milk to moisten, but keep batter stiff.

- Heat oil in deep fryer and carefully drop spoonfuls of batter into hot oil. Fry until golden brown. Remove and drain. Serves 4 to 6.

Southern Mint Jelly

1½ cups packed mint leaves
Green food coloring
1 (1.7 ounce) box fruit pectin
4 cups sugar
¼ cup lemon juice

- Pick out and wash fresh mint leaves. Place in saucepan with 3¼ cups water and heat to boil. Cover and steep for 10 minutes.

- Strain leaves and measure 3 cups liquid. Add few drops of green food coloring and pectin and bring to a boil. Add sugar and lemon juice and bring to a hard-rolling boil for 1 minute. Stir constantly.

- Remove from heat and skim foam off top. Pour immediately into hot, sterilized jars and seal. Yields 3 to 4 (8 ounce) jars.

Hush puppies are particularly popular in the South and often served with fried catfish. They are finger-shaped biscuit or muffin type bread made of cornmeal and deep-fried. Several stories are told about the origin of the name. One such story describes a slave who threw a plateful of the cornmeal mixture to a yelping dog to get him to stop making so much noise. Because it worked, the name Hush Puppies stuck. They are also called Corn Dodgers.

Bread-and-Butter Pickles

3 medium onions, sliced
30 (6 inch) cucumbers, sliced
3¾ teaspoons alum
6½ cups vinegar
5 cups sugar
1 tablespoon celery seed
2½ teaspoons mustard seed
1½ teaspoons turmeric
2½ teaspoons ground ginger

- Slice onions and cucumbers in bowl. Sprinkle 5 tablespoons salt and alum over both and let stand for 1 hour. Drain in colander and set aside.

- Make syrup of vinegar, sugar, celery seed, mustard seed, turmeric and ginger in large pot and bring to a boil for 5 minutes. Pour drained cucumbers into syrup.

- Place in hot, sterilized jars immediately and seal. Yields 5 to 6 (8 ounce) jars.

TIP: *Place jars in water and bring to a boil before filling so they will be hot enough to seal.*

Kentucky became the 15th state in 1792 and chose to be a commonwealth, building the government on the common consent of the people.

Okra Pickles

2 heads dill per pint jar
1 garlic clove per pint jar
1 pod hot pepper per pint jar
5 pounds young tender okra
1 tablespoon mixed pickling spices
8 cups vinegar
¾ cup salt, not iodized
¼ teaspoon alum per pint jar

- Place dill, garlic and hot pepper in sterilized jars. Pack in whole, washed okra.

- Measure pickling spices into piece of cheesecloth and tie with string for easy removal from syrup.

- Combine vinegar, salt, 1 cup water and spices in saucepan and bring to a boil. Pour over okra to fill jars and leave ¼ inch headspace from top of jar. Add alum to each jar. Seal immediately. Let stand for 8 weeks before using. Yields 6 pint jars.

Abraham Lincoln and Jefferson Davis, President of the Confederacy, were born in log cabins within one year and 100 miles of each other in south-central Kentucky.

Green Tomato Pickles

7 pounds green tomatoes
3 cups pickling lime
5 pounds sugar
3 pints vinegar
1 tablespoon ground cloves
1 tablespoon ground ginger
1 tablespoon ground allspice
1 tablespoon celery seed
1 tablespoon ground mace
1 tablespoon ground cinnamon

- Slice green tomatoes, but do not slice too thin. Dissolve lime in 2 gallons water in large pot, pour over tomatoes and soak for 24 hours. Stir often.

- Wash tomatoes in fresh water and soak in fresh water for 4 hours, but change water every hour.

- Boil sugar, vinegar and spices in saucepan; pour over tomatoes and let stand overnight.

- Next day, boil for 1 hour. Seal in hot, sterilized pint jars. Yields 6 to 8 pint jars.

Thomas Jefferson raised tomatoes in the 1780's and helped spread their popularity.

Watermelon Preserves

2 pounds watermelon rind, peeled, cubed
¼ cup pickling salt, not iodized
1 teaspoon powdered alum
2 cups white vinegar
4 cups sugar
1 lemon, thinly sliced
1 stick cinnamon
12 whole cloves
1 teaspoon whole allspice

- When peeling watermelon rind be sure to leave some of pink meat on.

- Make brine with pickling salt, 4 cups water and alum in large bowl. Soak rind in mixture overnight. Drain, rinse and cook slowly in fresh water in large pot until barely tender. Do not overcook or preserves will be too soft. Drain.

- Combine 2 cups water, vinegar, sugar, lemon and spices tied in cloth bag in large saucepan and bring to a boil. Remove spice bag and pour hot syrup over rind. Let stand overnight.

- Drain and reheat syrup for 3 mornings and pour over rind. On fourth morning, drain and reheat syrup and pour over rind packed in sterilized pint or half-pint jars. Seal. Yields 6 to 8 (8-ounce) jars.

Miss Sadie: *"There's just something about watermelon preserves that reminds me of my youth. Life was good."*

Chow-Chow

A delicious recipe to serve with meats and beans!

2 large heads cabbage
1½ pounds green bell peppers, chopped
4 red bell peppers, chopped
4 medium green tomatoes, chopped
4 medium onions, chopped
1½ pints vinegar
3 cups sugar

- Chop cabbage and add 4 teaspoons salt in bowl. Working with your hands, mix and squeeze until a bit of juice comes from cabbage.

- Add bell peppers and tomatoes. Work a bit more and add onions.

- Make syrup of vinegar, ½ cup water, 4½ teaspoons salt and sugar in saucepan. Let cool.

- Place chopped vegetable ingredients into cold syrup and bring to a rolling boil. Cook for 5 minutes after boil begins. Begin to put into hot, sterilized jars from center of pot. Do NOT cook too long or syrup will cook away. Seal. Yields 4 to 6 pint jars.

Miss Sadie: *"Now I need to tell y'all about chow-chow. If y'all have been so mistreated that y'all never tasted chow-chow, bless your hearts. We just put it on everything… black-eyed peas, lots o' vegetables and lots o' meat. Why, it's practically a side dish in the South."*

Fresh Veggies

Hot Casseroles

and

Fabulous Sides

Broccoli Casserole

2 (16 ounce) packages frozen broccoli spears, thawed
2 (10 ounce) cans cream of chicken soup
1 cup mayonnaise
4 teaspoons lemon juice
1 cup crushed herb dressing mix
¼ cup (½ stick) butter
1 (8 ounce) package shredded sharp cheddar cheese

- Preheat oven to 350°.

- Cook broccoli according to package directions. Cut cooked broccoli into bite-size pieces and arrange in 9 x 13-inch glass baking dish.

- Combine soup with mayonnaise and lemon juice in bowl and pour over broccoli. Brown crushed herb dressing in butter in skillet and layer over top of casserole. Sprinkle cheese on top and bake for 20 to 30 minutes until bubbly. Serves 12.

Skillet Cabbage

5 cups chopped cabbage
2 large onions, sliced
1 green bell pepper, chopped
2 tomatoes, chopped
1 tablespoon sugar
⅓ cup vegetable oil

- Combine all ingredients, 1 teaspoon salt and ½ teaspoon pepper in heavy skillet and cook over medium heat for 5 to 7 minutes or until tender. Serves 4 to 6.

Cabbage Casserole

1 head of cabbage
1 (10 ounce) can cream of celery soup
1 (10 ounce) package shredded cheddar cheese

- Preheat oven to 325°.

- Cut up cabbage and layer in 7 x 11-inch baking dish with celery soup and cheese. Bake for 35 minutes. Remove from oven and serve immediately. Serves 4 to 6.

Fried Fresh Corn

8 - 10 ears fresh corn
¼ cup (½ stick) butter
½ cup whipping cream
1 teaspoon sugar

- With sharp knife, slit kernel rows in half. Cut off top half of corn kernels into bowl. Once kernels are cut off, tilt cob into bowl to scrape remaining juice from kernels. (Position knife at an angle to scrape corn juice off cob.)

- Heat butter in heavy skillet and add corn. Stir rapidly until corn milk is thick, add cream and stir. Mix in a little salt and pepper and sugar. Cook mixture on low heat for 8 to 10 minutes or until mixture is thick. Serve immediately. Serves 6.

On April 25, 1866, a year after the Civil War, ladies of Columbus, Mississippi decorated Confederate and Union soldiers' graves at Friendship Cemetery with bouquets of flowers. It has been called "Where Flowers Healed a Nation". Their gesture resulted in what we now know as Memorial Day, celebrated annually in observance of fallen war heroes.

Miss Sadie: "Oh, honey. You haven't lived until you've eaten this fried corn! I guess if you're on one of those fancy diets, you could use milk instead of whipping cream. But, my goodness, it's just so good with that heavy cream."

Corn Fritters

¾ cup flour
1 teaspoon baking powder
1 tablespoon sugar
1 egg, well beaten
2 tablespoons milk
1 (11 ounce) can Mexicorn®, drained
Hot fat or oil

- Sift flour, baking powder, ½ teaspoon salt and sugar in bowl.

- In separate bowl, combine egg, milk and corn and add to flour mixture. Beat quickly and thoroughly.

- Drop tablespoonfuls of batter into deep fat heated to 360°. Fry fritters a few at a time until golden brown. Serves 6.

Corn Pudding

2 tablespoons flour
½ teaspoon white pepper
1 teaspoon sugar
3 eggs, well beaten
1 (15 ounce) and 1 (8 ounce) can whole kernel corn, drained
¼ cup (½ stick) butter, melted
1 (16 ounce) carton half-and-half cream

- Preheat oven to 325°.

- Combine flour, ½ teaspoon salt, white pepper and sugar in small bowl and set aside.

- In separate bowl, combine flour mixture, eggs, corn, butter (slightly cooled) and half-and-half cream. Mix well and pour into sprayed 2-quart baking dish.

- Cover and bake for 1 hour. Uncover and continue baking until top is delicate brown. Serves 8.

Nashville, Tennessee's Grand Ole Opry is known as the longest, continuously running, radio program in the world. It has been broadcast every weekend since 1925.

Parmesan Hominy

This makes a speedy side dish.

2 slices bacon, diced
2 tablespoons chopped onion
2 tablespoons chopped green bell pepper
1 (15 ounce) can hominy, drained
Seasoned salt
Grated parmesan cheese

- Fry bacon in skillet and cook just until still transparent. Add onion and bell pepper and cook until tender. Pour in hominy and add seasoned salt. Heat thoroughly and top with parmesan cheese before serving. Serves 4.

> *Hominy was a great gift from Native Americans to colonists in the New World. Today it continues to be a side dish in the South and throughout the country.*

Hominy was a great gift from Native Americans to colonists in the New World. Today it continues to be a side dish in the south and throughout the country.

Davy Crockett was born near the banks of Limestone Creek near Greenville, Tennessee, where a replica of his log cabin currently stands.

Mess o' Greens

A "mess of greens" usually means a big basket full or several
big handfuls of collard greens. You wash 'em, boil' em and
season 'em with a little ham hock or bacon and you've got a
real nice pot of greens ready to eat. You better eat some on New
Year's Day too because they bring you money in the New Year.

1 mess of collard greens
1 ham hock or thick-sliced bacon
½ teaspoon sugar

- Wash greens carefully to remove all dirt and grit. (It takes
  some doin'.) Place in large pot and add about 1 inch water.

- Add ham hock or bunch of bacon and boil. Add 1 teaspoon
  salt and sugar and cook on low until greens are tender.
  Serves 4.

Miss Sadie: *"Y'all need to know that a mess o'*
greens is really a couple o' big handfuls of anything
leafy and green. Why, I remember when my mama
would take me out in the field to pick poke sallet. It's
the poor people's greens, you know. She showed me
how to pick the smaller, young leaves because they were the only
ones that tasted good."

Supreme Green Beans

2 (15 ounce) cans French-style green beans, drained
1 (8 ounce) can sliced water chestnuts, drained
1 onion, chopped finely
2 tablespoons butter
2 teaspoons soy sauce
⅛ teaspoon hot sauce
2 tablespoons Worcestershire sauce
1 (10 ounce) can cream of mushroom soup
1 (8 ounce) package shredded sharp cheddar cheese
1 (3 ounce) can french-fried onions

- Preheat oven to 350°.

- Place green beans and water chestnuts in sprayed 2½-quart baking dish.

- Saute onion in butter in skillet and add 1 teaspoon salt, soy sauce, hot sauce, Worcestershire sauce, soup and cheese.

- Spoon mixture over green beans, cover and bake for 30 minutes.

- Uncover and sprinkle french-fried onions over top and return to oven for 10 to 15 minutes. Serves 8 to 12.

Southerners have a tradition of cooking "a mess o' greens" served with black-eyed peas on New Year's Day to bring good luck and money in the new year.

Fresh String Beans

2 - 3 pounds fresh green beans
3 tablespoons bacon drippings
2 teaspoons dried basil, optional

- Snap ends of green beans, wash and place in large saucepan.
  Pour about 1 inch water in pan and add bacon drippings,
  ½ teaspoon salt and basil. Bring to a boil, reduce heat
  and cover. Cook over low heat for 15 to 20 minutes.
  Serves 6 to 8.

Minted Peas

1 teaspoon dried mint leaves
Pinch of sugar
1 (10 ounce) package frozen tiny peas, thawed
Lump of butter

- Combine ½ cup water, mint, sugar, and a little salt and pepper
  in saucepan and bring to a boil. Add peas and cook for
  2 to 3 minutes. Drain slightly and add butter. Serves 4 to 6.

Primary agricultural crops in Alabama include
poultry, soybeans, milk, vegetables, wheat, cattle,
cotton, peanuts, fruit, hogs and corn.

Green Beans and Mushrooms

2 (16 ounce) packages frozen French-style green
    beans, thawed
1 onion, chopped
1 cup chopped pecans, divided
1 (10 ounce) cream of mushroom soup
1 (10 ounce) cream of chicken soup
6 large, fresh mushrooms, sliced

- Preheat oven to 375°.

- Cook green beans according to package directions and add onion. Drain and pour into sprayed 9 x 13-inch baking dish.

- Combine ½ cup pecans, soups and mushrooms in saucepan and heat but DO NOT COOK. Pour mixture over green beans and sprinkle with remaining pecans. Cover and bake for about 25 minutes. Serves 8 to 10.

Agriculture has always been a primary part of Mississippi's economy with farmers raising corn, rice, peanuts, pecans, sweet potatoes and sugar cane. Mississippi is the largest producer of pond-raised catfish in the U.S..

Stuffed Green Peppers

4½ bell peppers, divided
1 large onion
1 rib celery
½ bunch shallots
2 cloves garlic, minced
2 tablespoons butter
2 tablespoons fresh chopped parsley
½ pound ground beef
2 - 3 slices white bread
1 - 2 eggs as needed
1 carrot, grated
½ teaspoon sugar
1 cup seasoned breadcrumbs
Butter

- Preheat oven to 350°.

- Parboil 4 bell peppers for 3 minutes. Cut each pepper in half, remove seeds and membranes and cool; . Finely chop remaining ½ pepper, onion, celery and shallots. Place in saucepan and saute with garlic and butter. Add parsley and ground beef to mixture and cook until meat is well done. Remove from heat and set aside.

- Soak bread in ¼ cup water and 1 egg in bowl. Add bread and carrot to meat mixture and mix well. Add sugar and a little salt and pepper. If mixture is too stiff, add remaining egg.

- Fill bell pepper shells with meat mixture, cover with breadcrumbs and dot with butter. Bake for 30 to 40 minutes. Serves 6 to 8.

Creamed Peas and Mushrooms Elegant

4 slices bacon
¼ cup finely chopped onion
2 tablespoons flour
1 cup milk
1 (15 ounce) can green peas, drained
1 (4 ounce) can sliced mushrooms, drained
1 (2 ounce) jar diced pimientos
1 tablespoon butter
6 small, individual-size frozen piecrusts, baked

- Fry bacon in skillet until crisp. Remove, drain and crumble.

- Add onion to drippings in skillet and saute until tender. Pour off all but 1 tablespoon drippings. Blend in flour and add milk, ¼ teaspoon salt and a dash of pepper. Cook and stir until thick. Stir in peas.

- Saute mushrooms and pimientos in butter in saucepan and add to peas. Serve in individual-sized piecrusts. Serves 6.

Four of the first five presidents were from Virginia. A total of eight presidents were born in Virginia (George Washington, Thomas Jefferson, James Madison, James Monroe, William Henry Harrison, John Tyler, Zachary Taylor, Woodrow Wilson). However, William Henry Harrison moved to Ohio as a young man and was elected from that state.

Baked Acorn Squash

3 acorn squash
Grated nutmeg or ground ginger
6 teaspoons brown sugar, divided
6 teaspoons butter, divided
6 teaspoons sweet sherry, optional, divided

- Preheat oven to 325°.

- Split squash into halves and scoop out fiber and seeds. Sprinkle cavity of each half with a little nutmeg, a little salt and pepper, 1 teaspoon brown sugar, and 1 teaspoon butter

- Bake for 30 to 45 minutes or until flesh is tender. Add 1 teaspoon sherry to each cavity about 5 minutes before serving. Serves 6.

Iced tea is served year round in the South and is called sweet tea. Sweet tea is sweetened with sugar at the time it is brewed. South Carolina was the first and only state to produce tea and sell it commercially. In 1995, the South Carolina General Assembly adopted sweet tea as the Official Hospitality Beverage for the state.

Summer Squash Casserole

½ cup (1 stick) butter
1 (8 ounce) package herb dressing
2 pounds yellow squash, sliced, cooked, drained
2 small onions, finely chopped
1 (10 ounce) can cream of chicken soup
1 (4 ounce) can sliced water chestnuts
1 (2 ounce) jar diced pimientos

- Preheat oven to 350°.

- Melt butter in saucepan and stir into dressing. Divide and place half in 8 x 12-inch baking dish.

- Combine squash, onions, soup, water chestnuts and pimientos in bowl and pour over dressing. Cover with remaining dressing and bake for 30 to 40 minutes. Serves 8.

Battletown Inn Yellow Squash

7 small yellow squash, sliced
1 small onion, diced
¼ cup (½ stick) butter, divided
½ cup half-and-half cream
¾ cup saltine cracker crumbs, divided

- Preheat oven to 350°.

- Boil squash in salted water in saucepan until tender. Drain and mash.

- Saute onion in 2 tablespoons butter in skillet. Add half-and-half cream and ¼ cup cracker crumbs to onion and mix with squash.

- Pour into sprayed 1½-quart baking dish, top with remaining crumbs and dot with remaining butter. Bake for 30 to 45 minutes or until top is brown. Serves 4 to 6.

Squash Casserole

2 pounds yellow squash
1 large yellow onion, diced
2 cups seasoned breadcrumbs, divided
2 eggs, well-beaten
1 (8 ounce) package shredded colby and Monterey Jack
        cheese, divided
1 (8 ounce) carton whipping cream
1 teaspoon dried basil

• Preheat oven to 350°.

• Clean squash and slice. Place squash and onion in pot and
  cover with cold water. Add 1 teaspoon salt and bring to a
  boil. Reduce heat to medium and cook for about 15 minutes
  or until very tender. Drain well and place in large bowl.
  Fold in half breadcrumbs, eggs, half cheese and cream and
  mix well. Stir in basil and 1 teaspoon pepper.

• Pour into sprayed baking dish and sprinkle with remaining
  breadcrumbs and cheese. Cover and bake for 20 minutes.
  Uncover and return to oven for additional 10 minutes or
  until light brown on top. Serves 8 to 10.

Scalloped Okra and Corn

1 (15 ounce) can cut okra, drained
¼ cup (½ stick) butter, divided
1 (15 ounce) can whole kernel corn, drained
1 (10 ounce) can cream of celery soup
1 (8 ounce) package shredded sharp cheddar cheese
1 cup seasoned breadcrumbs

- Preheat oven to 350°.

- Stir-fry okra with 2 tablespoons butter in skillet for 10 minutes.

- Place okra in sprayed 7 x 11-inch baking dish and alternate with layers of corn.

- Heat soup in saucepan, stir in cheese and pour over vegetables. Cover with breadcrumbs and dot with remaining butter. Bake for 35 minutes or until breadcrumbs brown. Serves 6 to 8.

Okra Lovers' Fried Okra

2 eggs, lightly beaten
2 tablespoons milk
¾ cup cornmeal
¼ cup flour
22 - 28 fresh okra pods, thinly sliced
¼ cup vegetable oil

- Combine eggs and milk in shallow bowl and mix well.

- In separate bowl, combine cornmeal, flour and 1 teaspoon salt. Dip okra slices in egg-milk mixture and then in cornmeal mixture.

- Place okra in heavy skillet with hot oil and cook on medium-high heat until okra browns. Stir occasionally. Drain on paper towels. Serves 8 to 10.

Fried Green Tomatoes

1 pound green tomatoes
1 cup flour
1 - 2 tablespoons light brown sugar
Canola oil

- Cut ends off tomatoes, slice ⅓ inch thick and lay on paper towels to drain.

- Mix flour, brown sugar, and ½ teaspoon each of salt and pepper in shallow bowl.

- Dredge tomatoes in flour thoroughly. Heat oil in skillet and carefully place each slice in skillet. When 1 side of tomato is crispy and golden in color, turn to brown other side. Drain on paper towels and serve immediately. Serves 8.

TIP: *If you do most of your frying in a cast-iron skillet, add chopped onion to the skillet to absorb some of the tomatoes' acid. It will protect your skillet.*

Thomas Jefferson raised tomatoes in the 1780's and helped spread their popularity.

Baked Stuffed Tomatoes

6 large tomatoes
½ cup finely minced shallots
½ teaspoon garlic powder
2 tablespoons fresh chopped basil
¼ cup fresh minced parsley
½ teaspoon sugar
¼ teaspoon thyme
2 cups seasoned breadcrumbs
Olive oil

- Preheat oven to 400°.

- Cut tomatoes in half and seed. Sprinkle lightly with ¼ teaspoon salt and ⅛ teaspoon pepper. Place tomatoes in sprayed shallow baking dish.

- Combine shallots, garlic powder, basil, parsley, sugar, thyme and breadcrumbs in bowl. Fill tomatoes with mixture and drizzle with olive oil. Bake for 10 to 15 minutes. Serves 8.

Southern-Style Onion Rings

1 cup beer (not light beer)
1 cup flour
2 large yellow or Vidalia® onions
Vegetable oil

- Combine beer and flour in bowl, mix well and set aside for 3 to 4 hours (this is an important step).

- Slice onions into rings of desired width and dip in batter.

- Fry in hot oil deep enough to cover rings. Remove and drain on paper towels. As you cook onions, place them on shallow baking pan lined with brown paper. Keep hot in 200° oven. Serves 6 to 8.

Baked Vidalia Onions

1 large Vidalia® onion per person
1 tablespoon butter per onion
1 (8 ounce) package shredded sharp cheddar cheese, divided

- Preheat oven to 350°.

- Remove outer skin of onions. With sharp knife, remove very thin slice from bottom or root end of onion to allow onion to sit flat. Quarter onions, almost cutting down to core but not all the way.

- Insert butter into center slit of each onion. Add ½ teaspoon salt and ¼ teaspoon pepper to each onion and sprinkle heaping tablespoon cheese. Wrap onions individually in foil and bake for about 1 hour.

Scalloped Onions

6 yellow onions
¾ cup shredded cheddar cheese
½ teaspoon dried thyme
1 cup (2 sticks) butter, sliced
1 (8 ounce) carton whipping cream
1 cup seasoned breadcrumbs
⅓ cup grated parmesan cheese

- Preheat oven to 350°.

- Slice onions about 1 inch thick. Place in heavy pot with 1 inch or more of water to cover onions. Add 1 teaspoon salt and bring to a boil. Reduce heat, cover and simmer for 15 minutes. (Add a little more water if necessary to cover onions.)

- Drain onions and place half in sprayed baking dish. Sprinkle with ½ teaspoon salt, ¼ teaspoon pepper, cheddar cheese and thyme. Place butter slices over onions, add last layer of onions and pour cream over top. Sprinkle with breadcrumbs and parmesan cheese and bake uncovered for 35 minutes or until breadcrumbs are light brown. Serves 8 to 12.

In the fields around Vidalia and Glennville in southern Georgia, the granex seed produces one of the sweetest onions grown. The granex seed grown in many other parts of the U.S. produces a hotter onion. What makes the onion sweet in the Vidalia area is the low percentage of sulphur in the soil. There is a specific growing area defined by law. The Vidalia® onion was designated as the Official Vegetable of Georgia in 1990.

Vidalia Onion Sandwiches

Thin white bread
Mayonnaise
Vidalia® onions

- Cut out bread rounds about same diameter as onions. Coat amply with mayonnaise and top with very thin slice of onion. Sprinkle liberally with salt and pepper. Serve cold.

> ***Miss Sadie:*** *"I'll tell you a little secret. My favorite sandwich is as simple as can be. I cut 1 to 2 thick slices of a big garden tomato and a couple of big slices of a Vidalia onion (just the best in the world) and put them on some day-old white bread. Dab a little mayonnaise on that bread and take big ol' bites. With a glass of ice-cold sweet tea, I'm in heaven."*

Buttered Turnips

5 medium turnips, peeled, diced
2 teaspoons sugar
¼ cup (½ stick) butter, melted

- Combine turnips with sugar, 1½ teaspoons salt and ½ teaspoon pepper in saucepan and cook until tender. Rinse well, drain thoroughly and pour into serving dish. Add butter and mash. Serves 4 to 6.

Turnip Casserole

3 pounds turnips
¼ cup (½ stick) butter
1½ tablespoons sugar
3 eggs
1 cup seasoned breadcrumbs
1½ teaspoons lemon juice

- Pare and cut turnips into thin slices. Boil until tender, drain and mash hot turnips with butter, sugar, 1½ teaspoons salt and a little pepper. Beat until ingredients blend well.

- Add eggs one at a time and beat until fluffy. Stir in breadcrumbs and lemon juice. Pour into 1½-quart baking dish, cover and chill.

- When ready to bake, preheat oven to 375°.

- Bake for 50 minutes. Serves 8.

The Tennessee nickname of "The Volunteer State" came about during the War of 1812 when volunteer soldiers from that state displayed valor fighting in the Battle of New Orleans.

Zucchini Souffle

5 - 6 zucchini (about 2½ pounds) with peel
⅓ cup flour
4 large eggs
1 cup whipping cream
1 cup shredded Swiss cheese
½ teaspoon white pepper

- Preheat oven to 350°.

- Boil zucchini with peel in salted water in saucepan for 6 to 8 minutes. Drain well and puree in blender. Sprinkle flour on top, add 1½ teaspoons salt and remaining ingredients and mix well.

- Pour into sprayed 7 x 11-inch baking dish and bake for 45 minutes. If not brown at end of cooking time, place under broiler for several minutes. Set aside for 10 minutes before serving. Serves 6.

TIP: This is really easy and you can do part of it in advance.
Serve immediately and eat it all because it doesn't
freeze well.

Samuel Powhatan Carter was born in Elizabethton, Tennessee and is known in American history as the only person to be both a Navy Admiral and Army General.

Hoppin' John

This recipe (field peas over rice) is a southern dish and traditional on New Year's Eve and New Year's Day. The tradition is to eat field peas (black-eyed peas) for luck and collard greens for money in the coming New Year.

2 small onions, chopped
¼ cup (½ stick) butter
8 slices bacon, cut into pieces
1 cup cooked, cubed ham
1 cup rice
3 (15 ounce) cans black-eyed peas with liquid
Cayenne pepper

- Saute onion in butter in skillet for about 5 minutes and add bacon pieces. Cook until light brown. Add 2½ cups water and remaining ingredients to skillet and continue to cook over medium heat for 25 minutes until rice is tender. Serves 8 to 10.

Black-Eyed Peas

1 cup dried black-eyed peas
2 slices salt pork
1 medium onion, chopped
¼ teaspoon garlic powder

- Wash peas and place in large pot with 6 cups hot water. Add pork, onion, 2 teaspoons salt and garlic powder. Cover, bring to a slow boil and simmer over low heat for 2 hours 30 minutes or until tender. Drain before serving. Serves 6.

Barbecued Baked Beans

*These are not your ordinary beans and
they are great with barbecued pork!*

1 (15 ounce) can pork and beans
1 (15 ounce) can kidney beans, drained
1 (15 ounce) can green lima beans, drained
1 large onion, chopped
1 clove garlic, minced
1 tablespoon Worcestershire sauce
1 teaspoon ground cumin
2 - 3 tablespoons strong brewed coffee, cold
¼ cup packed brown sugar
½ cup ketchup
Pinch oregano
Pinch sweet basil
Dash hot sauce
3 bacon slices

- Preheat oven to 350°.

- Combine all ingredients except bacon slices in 9 x 13-inch
  baking dish. Place bacon slices on top. Cover and bake
  for 1 hour.

- Uncover and continue baking for additional 15 minutes.
  Serves 8 to 10.

*The Francis Beidler Forest near Charleston, South
Carolina claims the largest remaining virgin stand of
cypress and tupelo trees in the world.*

Twice-Baked Potatoes

2 large baking potatoes
Vegetable oil
2 tablespoons butter
2 tablespoons mayonnaise
1 tablespoon chopped chives
½ cup shredded cheddar cheese
Paprika

- Preheat oven to 375°.

- Scrub potatoes, rub skins with oil and bake for 1 hour. Allow potatoes to cool to touch. Cut potatoes in half lengthwise, scoop out flesh and leave shells intact.

- Mash flesh and combine with butter, mayonnaise, ¼ teaspoon salt, ⅛ teaspoon pepper and chives in bowl. Mix well and stuff shells with mixture. Sprinkle with cheese and paprika and place in shallow baking dish. Bake for 20 minutes. Serves 2 to 4.

"Hunley's Boat" was the first submarine used in warfare. Confederates used it in 1863 in Charleston Harbor.

Sweet Potato Souffle

3 cups cooked, mashed sweet potatoes
1 cup sugar
2 eggs, beaten lightly
3 tablespoons butter, melted
1 cup half-and-half cream
1 teaspoon vanilla

- Preheat oven to 350°.

- Combine sweet potatoes and sugar in bowl and mix well. Add ½ teaspoon salt and eggs and stir. Add butter, half-and-half cream and vanilla and stir.

- Pour sweet potato mixture into sprayed baking dish and bake for 35 minutes.

Topping:

⅓ cup (⅔ stick) butter
1 cup packed brown sugar
⅓ cup flour
1 cup chopped pecans
1 cup shredded coconut

- Melt butter in saucepan and add brown sugar, flour, pecans and coconut. Mix well. Spread mixture over top of baked sweet potatoes, return to oven and bake for additional 20 minutes. Serves 8.

Sweet potatoes are a great source of beta carotene; vitamins A, C and E; as well as dietary fiber. They are fat-free and cholesterol-free. And with all that, they have wonderful flavor and are easy to prepare.

Sweet Potato Balls

Looks like you worked all day, but no way!

2 cups crushed corn flakes, crushed
3 tablespoons plus 1 cup packed brown sugar, divided
1 (20 ounce) can sliced pineapple, drained
1 (28 ounce) can sweet potatoes or yams
¼ teaspoon lemon extract
1 teaspoon ground cinnamon
¼ teaspoon ground nutmeg
¼ cup (½ stick) butter, softened, divided
10 maraschino cherries

- Mix crushed corn flakes and 3 tablespoons brown sugar in shallow dish and set aside. Place 10 slices pineapple in sprayed baking sheet.

- Place sweet potatoes in bowl and mash with fork. Add 1 cup brown sugar, lemon extract, cinnamon, nutmeg and 2 tablespoons butter to sweet potatoes and beat until smooth. With your hands, form 10 balls of sweet potato mixture and roll in corn flake mixture until it coats well.

- Place sweet potato ball on pineapple slice and top with cherry. Chill until ready to bake.

- When ready to bake, preheat oven to 350°.

- Dot with remaining butter and bake for 25 minutes. Serves 10.

Miss Sadie: *"Sweet potatoes are just as good as they can be and good for you, too. They have lots of fiber and are just full of vitamins C and E. Now, take care of yourself."*

Brandied Sweet Potatoes

2½ pounds sweet potatoes
½ cup (1 stick) butter
½ cup packed light brown sugar
¼ teaspoon ground nutmeg
1 teaspoon ground cinnamon
½ cup brandy or sherry

- Preheat oven to 375°.

- Boil sweet potatoes in skins in saucepan until soft, drain and cool. Peel and slice crosswise about 1½-inch thick.

- Place in sprayed shallow baking dish and dot with butter.

- Combine brown sugar, nutmeg, cinnamon and ½ teaspoon salt in bowl and sprinkle mixture over potatoes. Pour brandy or sherry over all and bake for 30 minutes. Serves 6.

The sweet potato, a Southern favorite, is one of the most nutritious vegetables we have. They can be baked, grilled, sautéed, fried, boiled, steamed and eaten raw. They are served in appetizers, salads, side dishes, main dishes, breads and even desserts.

Short-Cut Cornbread Dressing

2 (8 ounce) packages cornbread mix
9 biscuits or 1 recipe biscuit mix
1 small onion, chopped
2 ribs celery, chopped
2 eggs
2 teaspoons poultry seasoning
3 (14 ounce) cans chicken broth, divided

- Prepare cornbread and biscuits according to package directions. Crumble cornbread and biscuits into large bowl. (Use a little more cornbread than biscuits.)

- Add onion, celery, eggs, a little pepper and poultry seasoning and stir in 2½ cans broth. If mixture is not runny, add remaining broth. (If it is still not runny, add a little milk.)

- Pour mixture into sprayed 9 x 13-inch baking dish and bake for 45 minutes or until golden brown. Serves 10 to 12.

Giblet Gravy

2 (14 ounce) cans chicken broth, divided
2 tablespoons cornstarch
2 eggs, hard-boiled, sliced, divided
Chicken or turkey giblets, cooked, chopped

- Mix ½ cup chicken broth with cornstarch in saucepan and stir until there are no lumps. Add remaining broth and a little pepper and heat to a boil and stir constantly until broth is thick. Add three-fourths egg slices.

- Add cooked giblets and pour into gravy boat. Garnish with remaining egg slices in saucepan. Serves 10 to 12.

Low Country Oyster Dressing

12 cups cubed day-old bread
2 cups chopped celery
1½ cups chopped onion
1 cup (2 sticks) butter
1½ pints oysters with liquor, chopped
3 eggs, beaten

- Place bread in large bowl. Saute celery and onion in butter in skillet and pour into bowl with bread.

- Drain liquor of oysters into small bowl. Mix chopped oysters, eggs and 1 teaspoon salt in bowl and pour into bread mixture. Use oyster liquor and milk to moisten mixture if needed. Serves 8 to 10.

Oyster-Cornbread Dressing

5 cups crumbled cornbread
4 cups toasted bread pieces
1 (14 ounce) can chicken broth
1½ cups chopped onion
1⅓ cups chopped celery
1 green bell pepper, chopped
2 tablespoons plus ½ cup (1¼ sticks) butter, divided
1 (16 ounce) carton raw oysters, drained, chopped
⅓ cup fresh chopped parsley
½ teaspoon sage
½ teaspoon thyme
2 eggs, beaten

- Preheat oven to 350°.

- Soak cornbread and bread pieces in chicken broth in bowl.

- Cook onion, celery and bell pepper in 2 tablespoons butter in saucepan until tender.

- Prepare oysters separately by simmering in saucepan with a little butter until edges curl. Remove from heat and drain well. Combine with breads, a little salt and pepper, remaining butter, and remaining ingredients.

- Use dressing to stuff turkey or shape into patties. Bake patties for 30 minutes. Serves 10 to 12.

Brown Rice Dressing

1 teaspoon rosemary
3 cubes chicken bouillon 3 teaspoons granules
1½ cups brown rice
6 slices bacon
½ cup diced green onions
2 tablespoons butter, melted
1 (8 ounce) can sliced water chestnuts

- Preheat oven to 325°.

- Combine 3 cups water, 1 teaspoon salt, rosemary and bouillon in saucepan and bring to a boil. Add brown rice, cover and simmer for 30 minutes or until all liquid absorbs into rice.

- Fry bacon in skillet until crisp and crumble into small pieces.

- Combine bacon, green onion, butter and water chestnuts in bowl and add to rice. Mix well and place in sprayed 7 x 11-inch baking dish. Cover and bake for 15 minutes. Serves 6.

Rice came to the South by way of a storm-ravaged merchant ship sailing from Madagascar and reaching the port of Charleston for safe haven. As a gift to the people, the ship's captain gave a local planter "Golden Seed Rice" and by 1700, rice was a major crop in the colonies. The success of the crop gave rise to the name "Carolina Gold Rice".

Three-Cheese Macaroni

1 (16 ounce) package macaroni
¼ cup (½ stick) butter, divided
1 (8 ounce) package longhorn cheese, cubed
1 cup cubed Swiss cheese
¼ cup grated parmesan cheese
1 tablespoon flour
1½ cups milk

- Preheat oven to 350°.

- Cook macaroni according to package directions. Drain and stir in half butter to keep macaroni from sticking together. While macaroni is still warm, mix in cheeses and stir until they melt. Pour mixture into sprayed 9 x 13-inch baking dish.

- Melt remaining butter in saucepan and add flour plus a little salt and pepper. Cook and stir for 1 minute. Slowly add milk and stir constantly. Cook until thick and pour over macaroni-cheese mixture.

- Cover and bake for 25 minutes. Uncover and continue to bake for additional 10 minutes. Serves 8.

Southern Macaroni and Cheese

1 (16 ounce) package shell pasta
2 tablespoons butter
3 eggs, beaten
1 (16 ounce) carton half-and-half cream
1 (12 ounce) package shredded cheddar cheese, divided
⅛ teaspoon cayenne pepper

- Preheat oven to 350°.

- Bring 4 to 5 quarts water to a boil in large pot. Add pasta and 2 teaspoons salt and cook for 6 minutes. (Pasta should be slightly undercooked.) Drain pasta and stir in butter to keep it from sticking. Transfer to sprayed 2½-quart baking dish.

- Combine eggs, half-and-half cream, three-fourths cheese and cayenne pepper in bowl and mix well. Pour mixture over pasta and sprinkle remaining cheese over top.

- Cover and bake for 35 minutes. Uncover and broil just enough to lightly brown top. Serves 8 to 10.

Macaroni and cheese is probably the ultimate comfort food and may have originated in the South. In Mary Randolph's The Virginia Housewife published in 1824, there is a recipe for macaroni and cheese. We know Thomas Jefferson returned from Europe with knowledge of macaroni and how to make it. Based on his interest in food, it is not inconceivable that he had some influence on the dish, particularly as he served it in the White House in 1802.

Grits You Will Love

2 tablespoons butter
1 small onion, chopped
⅛ teaspoon cayenne pepper
1 cup quick-cooking grits
¾ cup shredded cheddar cheese

- Preheat oven to 350°.

- Melt butter in saucepan and add onion. Cook onion for 3 minutes, pour in 3 cups water, ½ teaspoon salt and cayenne pepper and bring to a boil. Stir in grits and cook on medium heat for 2 minutes or until thick. Add cheese and mix well.

- Pour mixture into sprayed 2-quart baking dish and bake uncovered for 30 minutes or until brown on top. Serves 8.

Miss Sadie: *"Just so y'all understand one of the specialties of the South, I'll explain grits. We have fresh corn. We let that dry, and then call it hominy. We grind up hominy and call that grits."*

Garlic-Seasoned Grits

1 cup grits
1 (5 ounce) roll garlic cheese
½ cup (1 stick) butter
2 eggs
Milk

- Preheat oven to 350°.

- Cook grits in saucepan according to package directions. Add garlic cheese and butter and stir well.

- Beat eggs slightly, pour into measuring cup and add enough milk to equal 1 cup. Add to grits and mix well. Pour grits mixture into sprayed baking dish and bake for 30 minutes or until light brown on top. Serves 6 to 8.

Grits became the Official State Prepared Food of Georgia in 2002. They are made from bits of ground corn or hominy and are served as a breakfast dish or a side dish.

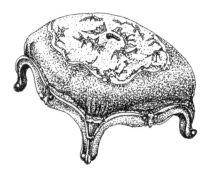

Slap-Yo'-Mama Main Dishes

More-Than-Burgers Beef

Chicken Lickin' Good

Pig Pickin' Pork Galare

Coastal Fresh, Tried and True Seafood Too

Feather, Fin and Game

Stuffed Cabbage

1 large head cabbage, cored
1½ pounds lean ground beef
1 egg, beaten
3 tablespoons ketchup
⅓ cup seasoned breadcrumbs
2 tablespoons dried, minced onion flakes
1 teaspoon seasoned salt
2 (15 ounce) cans Italian stewed tomatoes
¼ cup cornstarch
3 tablespoons brown sugar
2 tablespoons Worcestershire sauce

- Place head of cabbage in boiling water in large pot for 10 minutes or until outer leaves are tender. Drain well. Rinse in cold water and remove 10 large outer leaves. (To get that many large leaves, you may have to put 2 smaller leaves together to make 1 roll). Set aside.

- Take remaining cabbage and slice or grate in slivers. Place in sprayed 9 x 13-inch baking dish.

- Combine ground beef, egg, ketchup, breadcrumbs, onion flakes and seasoned salt in large bowl and mix well.

- Place ½ cup meat mixture packed together on each cabbage leaf. Fold in sides and roll leaf to completely enclose filling. You may have to remove thick vein from cabbage leaves for easier rolling. Place each rolled leaf over grated cabbage.

- Preheat oven to 325°.

- Place stewed tomatoes in large saucepan. Combine cornstarch, brown sugar and Worcestershire sauce in bowl and spoon mixture into tomatoes. Cook on high heat and stir constantly until tomatoes thicken. Pour over cabbage rolls, cover and bake for 1 hour. Serves 6.

Super Beef Casserole

1½ pounds lean ground beef
1 onion, chopped
1 (15 ounce) can tomato sauce
½ teaspoon dried basil
1 (8 ounce) package medium noodles
1 (16 ounce) carton small curd cottage cheese
1 (8 ounce) carton sour cream
1 cup shredded cheddar cheese

- Preheat oven to 350°.

- Brown beef and onion in large skillet and drain. Stir in tomato sauce, basil and ample amount of salt and pepper. Stir well and simmer for 25 minutes.

- Cook noodles according to package directions, drain and rinse in cold water. Spoon noodles into sprayed 3-quart baking dish.

- Combine cottage cheese and sour cream in bowl and spoon over noodles. Pour beef mixture over cottage cheese mixture and top with cheddar cheese. Bake for 25 to 30 minutes. Serves 8 to 10.

Daniel Boone is America's most famous pioneer and was responsible for much of the settlement of Kentucky. He improved the trails through the Cumberland Gap in the Appalachian Mountains and led his family and settlers to establish Fort Boonesborough in 1775. He improved the trail between the Carolinas and the center of Kentucky and it became known as the Wilderness Trail.

Miracle Meatloaf

*This is really good if you make it early in
the day or a day before you serve it.*

1½ pounds ground beef
¼ cup seasoned breadcrumbs
1 egg
2 cups mashed potatoes
2 eggs, hard-boiled, chopped
⅓ cup mayonnaise
⅓ cup grated parmesan cheese
¼ cup finely chopped celery
2 tablespoons sliced green onions

- Combine beef, breadcrumbs, egg and ½ teaspoon salt in
  bowl and mix well. Pat down beef mixture into 9 x 13-inch
  rectangle on foil or wax paper.

- Combine potatoes, hard-boiled eggs, mayonnaise, cheese,
  celery and green onions in bowl and mix lightly. Add a little
  salt and pepper and spread potato mixture over beef.

- Begin at narrow end and roll in jellyroll fashion. Chill
  several hours or overnight.

- When ready to bake, preheat oven to 350°.

- Bake on rack of sprayed broiler pan for 40 to 45 minutes.
  Serves 8.

Savory Pepper Steak

This is an easy way to fix steak!

¼ cup flour
1½ pounds round steak cut ½ inch strips
¼ cup vegetable oil
1 (15 ounce) can diced tomatoes, drained
½ cup chopped onion
1 small clove garlic, minced
1 tablespoon beef bouillon granules
1½ teaspoons Worcestershire sauce
2 large green bell peppers, seeded, julienned
Rice, cooked

- Combine flour, ½ teaspoon salt and ⅛ teaspoon pepper in bowl and coat steak.

- Brown meat on both sides with hot oil in large skillet. Add tomatoes, 1 cup water, onion, garlic and bouillon granules. Cover and let simmer for 1 hour 15 minutes or until meat is tender.

- Add Worcestershire sauce and bell peppers. Cover and simmer for additional 5 minutes. Thicken gravy with mixture of flour and cold water. Serve over rice. Serves 8 to 10.

Company Steak over Rice

1½ pounds round steak, cut into strips
Vegetable oil
2 onions, cut in ½ inch slices, separated into rings
1 (4 ounce) can sliced mushrooms, drained
1 (10 ounce) can cream of celery soup
1 (10 ounce) can beef broth
½ cup dry sherry
1 teaspoon seasoned salt
Rice, cooked

- Brown meat in a little oil in large skillet over high heat. Add onion, reduce heat and simmer for 5 minutes. Add mushrooms, soup, broth, sherry, seasoned salt and ample amount of pepper.

- Simmer on low heat for 1 hour or until steak is tender. Stir occasionally. Serve over rice. Serves 8.

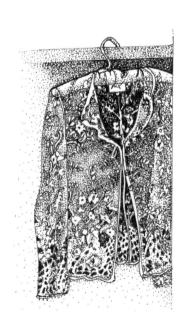

Smothered Fried Steak

6 cube steaks
Flour for dredging
Vegetable oil
1 large onion, sliced
1 (14 ounce) can beef broth

- Coat steaks well in flour heavily seasoned with salt and pepper. (Use remaining flour to thicken gravy later.)

- Heat oil in skillet and add steaks. Fry over medium-high heat and brown steaks on both sides. Add onion and saute for 10 minutes. Stir in beef broth and can of water and break up any scrapings from bottom of pan.

- Cover and allow steaks to simmer in liquid over low heat for 1 hour or until tender.

- When ready to serve, combine remaining flour (about ¼ cup) with a little water and add to steaks and gravy. Stir and heat until gravy is thick. Serves 6.

The Official State Beef Barbecue Championship Cook-Off in Georgia is called "Shoot the Bull Barbecue Championship", and is held each year in Hawkinsville.

Grilled Flank Steak

2 pounds flank steak
¼ cup soy sauce
⅓ cup honey
2 tablespoons cider vinegar
1½ teaspoons garlic salt
1 teaspoon ground ginger
¾ cup vegetable oil
1 small onion, finely minced

- Score steak about ¼ inch deep on each side and remove visible fat.

- Combine soy sauce, honey, vinegar, garlic salt, ginger, oil and onion in shallow bowl. Marinate steak overnight in refrigerator.

- Remove steak from marinade (discard marinade) and grill for 10 minutes on each side. Slice diagonally. Serves 8.

Miss Sadie: *"Do you know how much flank steak costs now? My, my, it used to be such a poor cut o' meat that it didn't cost much. Now, it's fancy."*

Southern Country Pot Roast

1 (4 pound) lean chuck roast
1 tablespoon paprika
2 tablespoons corn oil
1 bay leaf
2 large onions, peeled, quartered
1 (16 ounce) package baby carrots
4 large potatoes, peeled, quartered
1 (15 ounce) can tomato sauce
1 tablespoon dried parsley
1 (8 ounce) carton sour cream

- Preheat oven to 350°.

- Sprinkle roast with 2 teaspoons salt, ½ teaspoon pepper and paprika and place in roasting pan with hot oil. Brown on all sides. Add ¾ cup water and bay leaf.

- Cover and bake for 2 hours 30 minutes. Add onions, carrots, potatoes and tomato sauce; cover and bake for additional 1 hour.

- Remove roast from roasting pan and place on serving platter. Add parsley and sour cream to vegetables in roasting pan and stir well. Serve sauce over sliced roast and vegetables. Serves 10-12.

Pan-Fried Liver and Onions

Seasoned salt
Calf liver, sliced about ¼ inch thick
Flour
Canola oil
2 large onions

- Season calf liver slices and dredge with flour in shallow bowl. Brown both sides in small amount of oil in heavy skillet.

- Slice onions and separate into rings. Place rings on top of liver, cover and simmer for 20 minutes. Serve immediately.

TIP: *Fry a few strips of bacon crisp and set aside. Fry calf liver and onions in the bacon drippings instead of oil. Crumble bacon on top.*

Miss Sadie: *"I like to have bacon in this dish. When it's done, just crumble that bacon on top and you're in hog heaven."*

Barbecue in the South

Even though barbecue is considered a slow method of cooking over low fire or hot coals, in the South it is considered a social event. From the beginning when Native Americans taught settlers how to cure deer, settlers taught Indians how to smoke and cure meat, primarily pork.

Barbecue (the meat) always had a way of becoming a barbecue (an event). The settlers and Indians came together for celebrations. Plantation owners had neighborly parties, church members donated the pig and women brought covered dishes. Political rallies and speech-making always drew a better crowd with barbecue (and maybe a little bourbon).

Today barbecue has grown from farmers cooking back yonder behind the barn on weekends and selling their smoked meats at roadside stands to fancy barbecue joints with chairs, red and white checked vinyl tablecloths, and a smoky kind of ambience that makes it very approachable. Today barbecue is still a big event in the backyards of most Southerners.

Barbecue is a big deal in the South and most people identify the South with barbecue. The only real argument is what kind of meat and what kind of sauce goes on it. To most people in the South, pork is the only meat for barbecue. In some parts of Kentucky mutton was the preferred meat, but is now second to pork.

Barbecue in the South is a time-honored tradition and its roots are deep enough to keep it around for a long time. Just ask a Southerner what he thinks about barbecue and what is his favorite sauce. He won't mind telling you, but it will take some time.

Barbecued Brisket

1 (4 - 5 pound) trimmed beef brisket
3 ounces liquid smoke
Celery salt
Garlic salt
Onion salt
¼ cup Worcestershire sauce
¾ cup barbecue sauce

- Place brisket in oval baking dish and sprinkle with liquid smoke and seasoning salts. Cover and marinate in refrigerator overnight.

- When ready to bake, preheat oven to 275°.

- Sprinkle with Worcestershire sauce and a little salt and pepper. Place foil loosely over meat and cook for 5 hours. Pour barbecue sauce over meat. Increase heat to 325° and cook uncovered for additional 1 hour. Remove to platter and let cool before slicing. Serves 10 to 12.

The World Championship Barbecue Cooking Contest is held annually in Memphis, Tennessee in May. It is billed as the largest pork barbecue cooking contest on the planet.

Barbecued Spareribs

4 pounds spareribs
1 cup firmly packed brown sugar
¼ cup ketchup
¼ cup soy sauce
1 teaspoon dry mustard
½ cup chili sauce
¼ cup rum
¼ cup Worcestershire sauce
2 cloves garlic, crushed

- Preheat oven to 375°.

- Place ribs in baking pan, cover and bake for 30 minutes. Drain drippings.

- Combine remaining ingredients with a little pepper in bowl and pour over ribs.

- Reduce heat to 325° and bake uncovered for 1 hour 30 minutes. Baste occasionally. Serves 6.

TIP: This recipe can be used for grilling also.

The Slosheye Trail Big Pig Jig is the Official Georgia Pork Cook-Off and is held annually in Vienna, Georgia. It is considered the "Cadillac of barbecue contests" in the southeastern United States.

Barbecue Dry Rub

¼ **cup paprika**
2 - 3 **tablespoons light brown sugar**
2 **tablespoons chili powder**
2 **tablespoons cracked black pepper**
1 **tablespoon cayenne pepper**
1 **tablespoon ground cumin**
1 - 2 **tablespoons garlic powder**
1 **tablespoon celery salt**
1 - 2 **teaspoons dry mustard**

- Combine all ingredients with 1 tablespoon salt in bowl and mix thoroughly. Rub mixture into meat of your choice and wrap in plastic wrap. Chill for several hours or overnight. Yields 1 cup.

The Blossom Festival which features the World Championship Steak Cook-Off is held annually in Magnolia, Arkansas.

Barbecue Sauce

1 cup vinegar
⅔ cup lemon juice
2 teaspoons minced garlic
1 onion, finely grated
1 cup packed brown sugar
4 cups ketchup
1 teaspoon cayenne pepper
¼ cup mustard
2 teaspoons liquid smoke

- Combine vinegar, lemon juice, garlic, onion, and brown sugar in saucepan and bring to a boil. Add remaining ingredients and 1 tablespoon each of salt and pepper and boil for 5 minutes. Yields 1½ quarts.

The International Bar-B-Q Festival in Owensboro, Kentucky awards the Governor's Cup for the best barbecue.

Almond Chicken

4 boneless, skinless chicken breasts halves
3 tablespoons butter
1 (6 ounce) can frozen orange juice concentrate, thawed
2 tablespoons bourbon
Rice, cooked
½ cup chopped, salted almonds, toasted

- Season chicken with salt and pepper.

- Brown chicken in butter in skillet over medium heat;
  then reduce heat to low. Add orange juice concentrate, ½
  teaspoon salt and ¼ teaspoon pepper. Cover and cook over
  medium heat for 25 minutes. Spoon sauce over chicken
  twice while it cooks. Remove chicken to serving platter and
  keep warm.

- Add bourbon to sauce in skillet, stir and heat. Pour mixture
  over chicken and serve over hot, cooked rice. Sprinkle with
  almonds. Serves 4.

*The Kentucky Horse Park is located in Lexington
and features many exhibits, competitions and
activities. It is the site of the International Museum of
the Horse celebrating the 58-million year history of the
horse. It is the largest museum of its kind
in the world.*

Chicken Breasts Supreme

4 boneless, skinless chicken breast halves
¼ cup (½ stick) butter
1 (10 ounce) can cream of chicken soup
¾ cup sauterne or chicken broth
1 (8 ounce) can sliced water chestnuts, drained
1 (4 ounce) can sliced mushrooms, drained
2 tablespoons chopped green bell pepper
¼ teaspoon crushed thyme

- Preheat oven to 350°.

- Brown chicken breasts on all sides in butter in skillet. Arrange chicken in sprayed 9 x 13-inch pan. Sprinkle with ½ teaspoon salt and ⅛ teaspoon pepper.

- Add soup to butter in skillet and slowly stir in sauterne or broth. Add remaining ingredients and heat to a boil. Pour soup mixture over chicken.

- Cover and bake for 45 minutes. Uncover and bake for additional 15 minutes. Serves 4.

Chicken Divan

2 (10 ounce) packages frozen broccoli florets
4 boneless, skinless chicken breast halves, cooked, sliced
2 (10 ounce) cans cream of chicken soup
1 cup mayonnaise
1 teaspoon lemon juice
½ teaspoon curry powder or Worcestershire sauce
1½ cups shredded sharp cheddar cheese, divided
½ cup seasoned breadcrumbs
1 teaspoon butter, melted

- Preheat oven to 350°.

- Cook broccoli according to package instructions until tender and drain. Arrange broccoli in sprayed 9 x 13-inch baking dish. Place chicken slices on top.

- Combine soup, mayonnaise, lemon juice, curry powder or Worcestershire sauce and ¾ cup cheese in bowl and pour over chicken.

- In separate bowl, combine breadcrumbs and butter and layer over chicken. Sprinkle remaining cheese over top and bake for 25 to 30 minutes. Serves 4.

On August 5, 1864, at the Battle of Mobile Bay, Admiral David Farragut issued his famous command, "Damn the torpedoes, full speed ahead."

Chicken Souffle Special

Butter
16 slices white bread
6 boneless, skinless chicken breast halves, cooked, sliced
½ cup mayonnaise
1 cup shredded cheddar cheese, divided
5 large eggs
2 cups milk
1 (10 ounce) can cream of mushroom soup

- Butter bread slices on 1 side and remove crusts. Place 8 bread slices in sprayed 9 x 13-inch baking dish. Cover with chicken slices, spread with mayonnaise and sprinkle with ½ cup cheese. Top with remaining 8 slices bread.

- Beat eggs, milk and 1 teaspoon salt in bowl and pour over entire casserole. Chill overnight or 8 hours.

- When ready to bake, preheat oven to 350°.

- Spread soup over top and press down with back of spoon. Cover and bake for 45 minutes. Sprinkle with remaining cheddar cheese, return to oven and bake uncovered for additional 15 minutes. Serves 6.

TIP: You could use deli-sliced chicken instead of cooking chicken breasts.

Burial mounds found in Arkansas were a prominent feature of the region's last prehistoric culture called the Mississippian, which thrived from 800 A.D. to 1500 A.D.

Poppy Seed Chicken

6 boneless, skinless chicken breast halves
1 (10 ounce) can cream of chicken soup
1 (8 ounce) carton sour cream
½ cup dry white wine
1½ cups (1 stack) round buttery cracker crumbs
1 cup chopped almonds, toasted
½ cup (1 stick) butter, melted
2 - 3 tablespoons poppy seeds
Rice or noodles, cooked

- Preheat oven to 350°.

- Place chicken in sprayed 9 x 13-inch baking pan.

- Combine soup, sour cream and wine in saucepan and heat just until it mixes. Pour soup mixture over chicken.

- Combine cracker crumbs, almonds and butter in bowl and sprinkle over casserole. Sprinkle with poppy seeds and bake for 45 minutes. Serve over rice or noodles. Serves 6.

Succulent
Pecan-Chicken Breasts

⅓ cup (⅔ stick) butter
1 cup flour
1 cup finely ground pecans
¼ cup sesame seeds
1 tablespoon paprika
1 egg, beaten
1 cup buttermilk*
6 - 8 boneless, skinless chicken breast halves
⅓ cup coarsely chopped pecans
Fresh parsley or sage

- Preheat oven to 350°.

- Melt butter in 9 x 13-inch baking dish and set aside.

- Combine flour, finely ground pecans, sesame seeds, paprika, 1 teaspoon salt and ¼ teaspoon pepper in shallow dish.

- In separate bowl, combine egg and buttermilk. Dip chicken in egg mixture, dredge in flour mixture and coat well. Place chicken in baking dish and turn over to coat with butter. Sprinkle with coarsely chopped pecans and bake for 40 minutes or until golden brown. Garnish with fresh parsley or sage. Serves 6 to 8.

TIP: *Chicken may be cut into strips, prepared the same way and used as an appetizer. A honey-mustard dressing would be nice for dipping. This recipe could also be used for fish, like orange roughy, if cooking time is reduced to half.*

*TIP: *To make buttermilk, mix 1 cup milk with 1 tablespoon lemon juice or vinegar and let milk stand for about 10 minutes.*

Yummy
Barbecued-Grilled Chicken

6 boneless, skinless chicken breast halves
3 cups ketchup
½ cup packed brown sugar
¼ cup Worcestershire sauce
2 tablespoons vinegar
2 teaspoons seasoned salt
1 teaspoon hot sauce
½ teaspoon cracked black pepper

- Wash chicken breasts and dry with paper towels.

- Combine remaining ingredients in saucepan and mix well. Bring to a boil, reduce heat to low and cook for 15 minutes.

- Fire up grill and smoke chicken over mesquite wood, if possible. Baste chicken frequently with sauce. Turn chicken periodically and cook chicken for 8 to 10 minutes per side. Any leftover barbecue sauce keeps well in refrigerator. Serves 6.

One of the few remaining free-flowing rivers in the lower 48 states is the Buffalo River in Arkansas. It was declared the first National River in 1972.

Tootsie's Chicken Spectacular

2 cups cooked, diced chicken
1 (15 ounce) can green beans, drained
1 cup cooked rice
1 (10 ounce) can cream of celery, chicken or mushroom soup
½ cup mayonnaise
½ cup sliced water chestnuts
2 tablespoons diced pimientos
2 tablespoons chopped onion

- Preheat oven to 350°.

- Combine all ingredients with ¼ teaspoon salt and a dash of pepper in bowl and mix well. Place in sprayed 1½-quart baking dish and bake for 25 to 30 minutes. Serves 4 to 6.

TIP: This is a great recipe for leftover turkey.

The oldest Mardi Gras celebration in the country was introduced in Mobile, Alabama. It is a celebration held on Shrove Tuesday, the Tuesday before Lent.

Chicken Elegant

This is rich, but worth the calories!

3 tablespoons butter
3 tablespoons flour
1¾ cups milk
½ cup shredded sharp American cheese
½ cup shredded Swiss cheese
½ teaspoon Worcestershire sauce
1 cup cooked, diced chicken or turkey
1 cup cooked, diced ham
1 (4 ounce) can sliced mushrooms, drained
2 tablespoons diced pimientos
Toast points or noodles, cooked

- Melt butter in saucepan and blend in flour. Add milk all at once; cook and stir until sauce is thick and bubbly. Remove from heat, add cheeses and stir until they melt.

- Stir in Worcestershire sauce, chicken, ham, mushrooms and pimientos. Heat thoroughly and serve over toast points or noodles. Serves 8 to 10.

The oldest state-funded archival agency in the nation is the Alabama Department of Archives.

Tasty Chicken Casserole

1 onion, chopped
1 cup sliced celery
3 tablespoons butter
4 cups cooked, diced chicken
1 (6 ounce) package long grain-wild rice with seasoning
  packet, cooked
1 (10 ounce) can cream of celery soup
1 (10 ounce) can cream of chicken soup
1 (4 ounce) jar pimientos, drained
2 (15 ounce) cans French-style green beans, drained
1 cup slivered almonds
1 cup mayonnaise
2½ cups crushed potato chips

- Preheat oven to 350°.

- Saute onion and celery with butter in small saucepan
  and pour into larger saucepan with chicken, rice, soups,
  pimientos, green beans, almonds, mayonnaise, ½ teaspoon
  salt and 1 teaspoon pepper.

- Pour into sprayed 10 x 15-inch baking dish. (This recipe
  needs a very large baking dish.)

- Sprinkle crushed potato chips over casserole and bake
  for 35 minutes or until potato chips are slightly brown.
  Serves 12 to 14.

Old-Fashioned Chicken Spaghetti

8 - 10 ounces spaghetti
1 bell pepper, seeded, chopped
1 onion, chopped
1 cup chopped celery
½ cup (1 stick) butter
1 (10 ounce) can tomato soup
1 (10 ounce) can diced tomatoes and green chilies
1 (4 ounce) can chopped mushrooms, drained
½ teaspoon garlic powder
3 teaspoons chicken bouillon granules
4 - 5 cups chopped chicken
1 (8 ounce) package cubed Velveeta® cheese
1 (8 ounce) package shredded cheddar cheese

- Preheat oven to 325°.

- Cook spaghetti according to package directions and drain.

- Saute bell pepper, onion and celery with butter in medium saucepan. Add soup, tomatoes and green chilies, mushrooms, ½ teaspoon each of salt and pepper, garlic powder, bouillon granules, and ½ cup water and mix.

- Combine spaghetti, vegetable-soup mixture, chicken and cheeses in large bowl.

- Place in 2 sprayed (2 quart) baking dishes. Freeze one; cover and bake the other for 40 to 50 minutes. To cook frozen casserole, thaw first. Serves 10.

TIP: This is a good recipe for leftover turkey.

Southern Fried Chicken

1 whole chicken, cut up
2 eggs, beaten
2 tablespoons cream
Flour
Vegetable oil or shortening

- Wash chicken pieces and dry with paper towels. Sprinkle all sides with salt and pepper.

- Combine eggs and cream in bowl. Dip chicken into egg mixture, dredge in flour and coat well.

- Carefully place chicken in heavy skillet with ¼ inch heated oil or shortening and cover. Brown chicken pieces over medium heat on both sides. Lower heat and cook for 25 minutes or until tender.

Gravy:

3 tablespoons flour
1½ cups milk

- Remove chicken from skillet and add flour and ½ teaspoon each of salt and pepper and stir constantly. Increase heat to high. Add milk, cook and stir until gravy is thick. Serve hot. Serves 8.

Miss Sadie: *"Honey, if you want to make someone happy just learn how to cook good fried chicken!"*

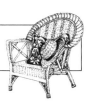

Deep-Fried Chicken

1 whole chicken, cut up
1 cup flour
2 eggs
2 cups milk
1 teaspoon lemon juice
Vegetable oil

- Wash chicken and pat dry with paper towels. Season chicken with salt and pepper.

- Combine flour, eggs, milk and lemon juice in bowl and mix thoroughly.

- Dredge chicken in batter and fry in deep fryer with oil over medium-high heat until golden brown. Serves 6.

Milk Gravy

3 - 4 tablespoons bacon drippings
⅓ cup flour
1½ cups milk

- After frying bacon, pour drippings off and leave 3 to 4 tablespoons drippings in skillet. Add flour to skillet and add liberal amounts of salt and pepper.

- Cook and stir until flour is light brown. Slowly add milk and stir constantly. Cook until mixture is thick. Serves 6.

Roasted Chicken Supreme

This is such an easy recipe and good for any meal.

1 (3 pound) whole chicken
1 rib celery
1 onion
Vegetable oil
Paprika

- Preheat oven to 325°.

- Wash chicken and dry with paper towels. Cut celery rib in half. Insert onion and celery into chicken cavity. Tie legs, rub chicken with oil and sprinkle with paprika.

- Roast in open pan for 35 minutes per pound of chicken. Baste every 40 minutes. To serve, remove onion and celery. (You can save and use for soup or stew.) Chicken will be extra juicy and moist with no onion flavor. Serves 8.

Sweet grass basket-making has been going on in the Mount Pleasant community in South Carolina's Low Country for more than 300 years. It is a traditional art form that has been passed down for several generations.

Finger-Lickin' Smoked Chicken

3 whole chickens, halved
Seasoned pepper
½ cup (1 stick) butter
2 teaspoons Worcestershire sauce
2 dashes hot sauce
2 tablespoons lemon juice
½ teaspoon garlic salt
1 cup (8 ounces) 7UP®

- Sprinkle chickens with seasoned pepper and leave at room temperature for 1 hour.

- Melt butter in small saucepan and add Worcestershire sauce, hot sauce, lemon juice, garlic salt and 7UP®.

- Cook chickens on grill using mesquite charcoal. Turn often and baste with sauce mixture several times. Grill for about 1 hour and baste once more to keep chicken moist. Serves 6 to 10.

The Cumberland Gap National Historical Park in Kentucky, Virginia and Tennessee is the largest national historical park in the U.S. With more than 20,000 acres of wilderness, 80% of the park has no paved roads. Majestic vistas may be seen from more than 70 miles of hiking trails and at the eastern end of the park it is possible to see the Great Smoky Mountains more than 80 miles away.

Old-Fashioned Chicken and Dumplings

2 pounds boneless, skinless chicken breasts
½ onion, chopped
½ cup sliced celery
1 carrot, sliced
3 tablespoons shortening
2 cups flour

- Place chicken breasts in large soup pot and cover with water. Add onion, celery, carrot, 1 teaspoon salt and ½ teaspoon pepper.

- Cover and cook for 40 minutes or until chicken is tender. Remove chicken and break into bite-size pieces. Strain broth and return broth and chicken to large pot.

- Cut shortening into flour and 1 teaspoon salt with pastry blender or fork in large bowl until dough is pea-size. Add 9 tablespoons ice water, 1 tablespoon at a time, and mix lightly with fork.

- On floured surface, roll dough very thinly and keep rolling pin well floured. Cut into strips and lay on wax paper. Chill for 45 minutes.

- Bring broth and chicken pieces to a boil. Drop strips into boiling broth and chicken pieces. Do not stir but jiggle or shake pot. (Stirring will break up dumplings.) Cook on medium heat for 30 minutes. Serves 8.

Family Secret Chicken and Noodles

This is a great recipe to prepare ahead of time and freeze.

¼ cup (½ stick) butter
½ cup flour
½ teaspoon basil
½ teaspoon parsley
1 pint milk
1 (4 ounce) can sliced mushrooms, drained
1 (10 ounce) can cream of mushroom soup
1 (2 ounce) jar diced pimientos
1 (4 pound) stewing hen, cooked, diced
1 (14 ounce) can chicken broth
1 (16 ounce) package medium egg noodles
4 ounces shredded cheddar or American cheese
Paprika

- Melt butter in saucepan over medium heat and add flour, basil, parsley and ½ teaspoon salt. Add milk slowly and stir constantly until thick.

- Add mushrooms, soup, pimientos, chicken and chicken broth.

- Cook noodles according to package directions. Drain. Mix noodles with sauce and stir gently.

- Pour mixture into sprayed 9 x 13-inch baking dish. Sprinkle with cheese and paprika. Cover and chill until baking time.

- When ready to bake, preheat oven to 350°.

- Bake for 20 to 30 minutes until it is thoroughly hot. Serves 8 to 10.

Cranberry-Glazed Cornish Hens

6 cornish hens, thawed
1 (16 ounce) can whole cranberry sauce
¼ cup (½ stick) butter
¼ cup frozen orange juice concentrate, thawed
2 teaspoons grated orange peel
Pinch of poultry seasoning
1 tablespoon brown sugar

- Preheat oven to 400°.

- Wash hens under cold water. Pat dry with paper towels and season with salt and pepper inside and out. Place hens in shallow pan without rack and bake for 35 minutes.

- Heat cranberry sauce, butter, orange juice concentrate, orange peel and poultry seasoning in saucepan. Pour mixture over hens.

- Lower oven temperature to 350° and continue to bake for additional 30 minutes. Baste often with cranberry sauce until it browns well.

- Sprinkle brown sugar lightly over hens and slip under broiler to glaze. Serves 6.

Southern Stuffed Peppers

6 large green bell peppers
½ pound chicken livers, chopped
6 slices bacon, diced
1 cup chopped onion
1 cup sliced celery
1 clove garlic, crushed
1 (4 ounce) can sliced mushrooms
2 cups cooked rice
Dash of cayenne pepper

- Wash peppers, cut slice from stem end and remove seeds. Cook peppers for about 5 minutes in small amount of boiling salted water in large saucepan. Remove from water and drain.

- Cook chicken livers, bacon, onion, celery and garlic in skillet until vegetables are tender. Add mushrooms, rice, cayenne, 1 teaspoon salt and ¼ teaspoon pepper. Stuff peppers with mixture.

- Arrange in baking pan, seal and freeze. Thaw before baking.

- When ready to bake, preheat oven to 375°.

- Add ½ inch water to pan, cover and bake for 20 to 25 minutes. Serves 6.

The Atlantic Flyway is a route for birds migrating along the Atlantic coast. It crosses Virginia and the state protects important resting and feeding grounds.

Turkey Croquettes

*These are very easy to make. Make several
batches and freeze them for another meal.*

1½ cups cooked, chopped turkey
1 (10 ounce) can cream of chicken soup
1 cup turkey stuffing mix
2 eggs
1 tablespoon minced onion
Flour
Vegetable oil

- Mix turkey, soup, stuffing mix, eggs and onion in bowl and
  chill for several hours.

- Shape into patties or rolls. Dredge in flour and fry in hot oil
  until brown. Serves 6 to 8.

*The first permanent British settlement, Jamestown,
Virginia was founded for the purpose of silk
cultivation for trade with the court of King James.
After fungus destroyed the mulberry trees, tobacco was
planted as a cash crop.*

Smoked Turkey

*This may sound incredible, but it works! The trick is
teaching your husband to smoke the turkey! Thanksgiving
is much more enjoyable with a "little help in the kitchen"!*

1 butter-basted turkey
1 onion, peeled, halved
2 - 3 small ribs celery
Poultry seasoning
2 - 3 strips bacon

- Buy turkey that will fit on covered grill. Soak hickory chips
  in water while charcoal gets "good and hot". Place washed
  and dried turkey in disposable aluminum foil roasting pan.

- Rub poultry seasoning, salt and pepper on turkey inside and
  out and insert onion and celery in cavity of turkey. Lay strips
  of bacon across top of turkey.

- Pour a little water in pan to prevent sticking and place on
  grill. Close grill cover and cook for 11 minutes per pound.
  Baste occasionally during cooking time. (This cooking
  method produces a beautiful brown turkey. The meat
  will look slightly pink due to the smoking procedure,
  but it is done!)

- Pan drippings in roaster are ready to make gravy. By using
  this procedure, Thanksgiving cooking is much easier because
  your oven is free for other dishes. Just throw away the messy
  pan when you are finished! (You can discard the onion and
  celery or use them later in soup, etc.) Serves 8.

Pork Chops
and Red Cabbage

6 (1 inch) thick pork chops
Vegetable oil
⅓ cup flour
⅓ cup sugar
½ cup cider vinegar
1 small red cabbage, shredded
2 Rome apples, with peel, sliced

- Brown pork chops on both sides with a little oil in skillet. Lower heat, cover and simmer for 15 minutes.

- Combine flour, sugar, and liberal amount of salt in bowl.

- In separate bowl, combine vinegar and ¼ cup water.

- In larger bowl, combine cabbage and apples and toss with flour-sugar mixture and then vinegar mixture. Spoon over pork chops, cover and simmer for 30 minutes. Serves 6.

Colonists of Virginia brought pigs from England as a source of food. Native Americans taught the colonists their methods for curing venison and the settlers adapted the salting, smoking and aging to hams.

Pan-Fried Pork Chops

Look for Miss Sadie's comment for another
step to these wonderful pork chops.

6 - 8 thin pork chops
¾ cup flour
¼ cup extra-virgin olive oil

- Salt and pepper pork chops and dredge in flour. Pat flour into pork chops so it will stick.

- Carefully place pork chops into skillet with hot oil and brown on both sides. Make sure center cooks well. Serves 6 to 8.

TIP: *Brown pork chops in ovenproof skillet, add a little water and bake in oven for 45 minutes at 350°.*

Miss Sadie: *"I always pan-fried my pork chops and I always had people coming back. One day after I cooked those pork chops, I added a little water to my lovely cast-iron skillet, fit all those chops in the skillet and baked them in the oven and those pork chops just fell apart."*

Pork Chop Casserole

¾ cup rice
6 pork chops, floured
2 tablespoons vegetable oil
1 large onion, chopped
1 medium bell pepper, cut in rings
1 (15 ounce) can diced tomatoes
¼ teaspoon thyme
¼ teaspoon marjoram
1 (10 ounce) can beef broth

- Preheat oven to 350°.

- Place rice in 2-quart shallow baking dish. Brown floured chops in oil in skillet and place on top of rice.

- Brown onion and bell pepper in remaining oil and pour over pork chops.

- Combine tomatoes, thyme, marjoram and 1 teaspoon salt in bowl and pour over pork chops. Pour beef broth over entire casserole. Cover and bake for 1 hour. Serves 6.

Chitlins (originally chitterlings) is the informal name given to the intestines of hogs cooked for human consumption. They originated with slaves who were given leftovers when hogs were butchered.

Barbecued Pork Chops

6 pork chops
1 tablespoon chili powder
1 teaspoon paprika
¼ cup packed brown sugar
½ cup vinegar
1 (10 ounce) can tomato soup

- Preheat oven to 350°.

- Place pork chops in baking dish.

- Combine remaining ingredients with 1 teaspoon salt in bowl and pour over chops. Bake for 1 hour 30 minutes. Serves 6.

Miss Sadie: "Southerners know how to cook barbecue and don't you let anyone tell you different."

Pork Loin with Apricot Glaze

1 (3½ - 4 pound) center-cut pork loin
1 tablespoon olive oil
Seasoned pepper
1 teaspoon dried rosemary
1 cup dry white wine
1½ cups apricot preserves

- Preheat oven to 350°.

- Rub loin with olive oil and sprinkle seasoned pepper and rosemary over top. Place in shallow roasting pan, pour wine and 1 cup water over loin and bake for 1 hour.

- Remove from oven and spoon 1 cup pan drippings into small bowl. Add apricot preserves to drippings and mix well. Pour apricot mixture over pork in pan, turn oven to 325° and return to oven. Continue to cook for additional 1 hour and baste 2 to 3 times with pan drippings. Remove from oven and set aside to cool for 15 minutes before slicing.

- To cook day before, cook as directed and let roast cool. Take roast out of drippings, place in glass baking dish and slice. Place drippings in separate container and chill both. When ready to serve, heat drippings and pour over roast. Warm in oven at 350° for 20 minutes. Serves 8.

Grilled Pork Loin

½ **teaspoon garlic powder**
¼ **teaspoon celery salt**
½ **teaspoon onion salt**
2 **tablespoons lemon juice**
1 **(5 pound) pork loin**

- Combine garlic powder, celery salt, onion salt and lemon juice in bowl. Rub mixture into loin and place in covered glass dish. Chill for at least 8 hours or overnight.

- Grill loin over hot coals for 30 minutes or until thickest portion of meat reaches 140°. (Center part of tenderloin will be slightly pink.) Set aside for at least 10 minutes before cutting. Serves 8 to 10.

The annual Newport Pig Cookin' Contest is the largest whole hog cooking contest in the U.S. It is held in April in Newport, North Carolina.

Carolina Pulled Pork

*Lots of people in the South eat their coleslaw
right on the bun with the pork. It's great!*

4 onions, divided
1 (3 - 4 pound) pork roast or shoulder
Carolina-style barbecue sauce with mustard
Buns
Coleslaw
Dill pickles

- Slice 1 onion into rings and place in bottom of slow cooker
  and place roast on top. Slice another onion into rings and
  place over top of roast; fill slow cooker about half way or a
  little more with water. Cook over LOW heat overnight.

- Remove roast and pour out all but 1 to 2 inches liquid from
  slow cooker. When roast is cool, pull meat apart with fingers
  or shred it with fork. Return roast to slow cooker and pour
  barbecue sauce over meat.

- Chop 1 onion, season with salt and pepper and add to meat.
  Cook on HIGH for several hours until onion is tender.
  Serve on large buns with coleslaw, dill pickles and slices of
  remaining onion. Serves 8 to 12.

TIP: *If your barbecue sauce is thick, you may need a little more
     liquid from slow cooker so meat will not be dry.*

*The Virginia variety of peanut is the one used
for roasting because it has the largest kernels. This
variety is grown mostly in southeastern Virginia and
northeastern North Carolina.*

Barbecued Pork Roast

3 onions, divided
5 pound pork roast, boned, trimmed
6 whole cloves
1 (16 ounce) bottle barbecue sauce
Buns

- Slice 2 onions and place half onion slices in slow cooker. Add meat, cloves and 2 cups water; top with remaining sliced onions. Cover and cook overnight or for 8 to 12 hours on LOW.

- Discard drippings. Remove and shred meat. Chop remaining onion. Return meat to slow cooker along with chopped onions and barbecue sauce. Cook on HIGH for 2 hours and stir occasionally. Serve roast on buns. Serves 10 to 12.

Lexington, North Carolina considers itself the Barbecue Capital of the World. Its annual Barbecue Festival is held in October.

Ginger Baby Back Ribs

1 tablespoon butter
1 onion, chopped
1 cup apricot preserves
¼ cup soy sauce
¼ cup honey
3 tablespoons red wine
1 tablespoon fresh grated ginger
1 tablespoon dried orange peel
4 - 5 pounds baby back pork ribs

- Preheat oven to 375°.

- Melt butter in saucepan and cook onion until tender, but not brown. Add apricot preserves, soy sauce, honey, wine, ginger and orange peel. Cook and stir constantly until mixture heats thoroughly.

- Place ribs in large baking pan and pour preserves mixture over ribs.

- Cover and bake for 30 minutes. Reduce heat to 275° and bake 3 hours to 3 hours 30 minutes or until rib meat is tender. (If ribs have not browned, remove cover and bake for additional 15 minutes.) Serves 6 to 8.

The World Championship Barbecue Cooking Contest is held annually in Memphis, Tennessee, in May. It is billed as the largest pork barbecue cooking contest on the planet.

Low Country Boil

3 pounds kielbasa or link sausage
4 potatoes with peels
3 onions
3 cups cut green beans, drained

- Cut sausage into bite-size pieces. Wash potatoes and peel onions.

- Place sausage, potatoes, whole onions and green beans into large stockpot, cover with water and boil until potatoes are tender. Season according to your own taste. Serves 8 to 10.

Savory Sausage and Sweet Potatoes

1 pound sausage
2 large sweet potatoes, peeled, sliced
3 Granny Smith apples, peeled, sliced
⅓ cup sugar
1 tablespoon flour

- Preheat oven to 350°.

- Form sausage into small balls and fry in skillet until well done. Drain sausage.

- Arrange potatoes, apples and sausage balls in layers in sprayed 2-quart baking dish.

- Combine sugar, flour and ½ cup water in bowl and mix well. Pour mixture over layers. Cover and bake for 40 minutes or until potatoes are tender. Serves 6.

Sausage Souffle

8 slices white bread, cubed
2 cups shredded sharp cheddar cheese
1½ pounds link sausage cut in thirds
4 eggs
2¼ cups milk
¾ teaspoon dry mustard
1 (10 ounce) can cream of mushroom soup
½ cup milk

- Place bread cubes in sprayed 9 x 13-inch baking dish and top with .

- Brown sausage in skillet and drain. Place sausage on top of cheese.

- Beat eggs with milk and mustard in bowl and pour over sausage. Cover and chill overnight.

- When ready to bake, preheat oven to 300°.

- Dilute soup with milk and pour over bread and sausage. Bake for 1 hour or until set. Serves 8 to 10.

Sweet potatoes are high in vitamins C and E and beta carotene, a form of vitamin A. Beta carotene is the source of yellow, red and orange pigments in fruits and vegetables. It is an extremely important nutrient needed to maintain good health and to reduce the risk of disease.

Smithfield Virginia Country Ham

Smithfield Country Hams are the most famous in the U.S. and can only be cured in Smithfield, Virginia.

1 Smithfield Virginia Country Ham

When you first unwrap a country ham, you may think something is wrong with it because the outside is covered in mold. When hams are aged, mold is part of the process, but is in no way harmful to the ham or to you.

Wash and scrape off this outside coating of mold with warm water. Soak ham for about 12 to 24 hours to pull out some of the salt in the ham. (Change water several times to pull out more salt.) Cook the country ham in one of the following ways.

Boiling:

- Place ham skin-side down in large roasting pan and cover with water. Cook in simmering hot water (not boiling) for 25 minutes per pound or until internal temperature reaches 160°.

- Add water if necessary to keep ham covered. Remove ham from roasting pan and remove outside skin and fat.

- Serve as is or sprinkle brown sugar, honey or molasses, and breadcrumbs on the outside and bake in oven at 400° until outside is brown. Carve into thin slices and serve immediately.

Continued next page...

Continued from previous page...

Roasting:

- Preheat overn to 300°.

- Wrap ham in foil with opening at top and place in large baking pan. Pour 4 cups water into foil and seal. Bake for 20 minutes per pound or until meat thermometer reaches 160°.

- Remove from oven and scrape off outside skin and fat. Carve into thin slices and serve.

Pan Fry:

- Carve ham into very thin slices and fry in large skillet with a little oil over medium low heat for about 10 to 15 minutes or until ham slice is cooked throughout. Serve immediately.

Slicing:

"Start slicing several inches away from hock or small end. Make first slice straight through to the bone. Slant the knife for each succeeding cut. Decrease slant as slices become larger."

—www.smithfield.com

The tradition of cured, smoked country ham began in Smithfield, Virginia in the mid 1700's. The back part of a pig's thigh was salted, seasoned, smoked and aged to create one of the real delicacies of the South. Today Virginia country hams are considered some of the best in the world, but if you ask someone from Tennessee, Kentucky, North Carolina or Georgia, you will surely get an argument. Hams are usually slow-smoked with hickory, apple or pecan wood, salted, seasoned with pepper and cured for 10 to 12 months.

Carolina Country Ham

1 smoked ham
1 apple
1 onion
1 cup molasses
1 teaspoon mixed pickling spices
½ cup packed brown sugar
1 teaspoon Worcestershire sauce
1 (20 ounce) can pineapple slices, drained
Whole cloves

- Soak ham overnight and clean thoroughly. Place ham in large container and cover with cold water. Add apple and onion. Pour in molasses and pickling spices. Simmer slowly for about 20 minutes per pound of ham.

- Remove ham from heat just before meat falls off bone and cool in water. Skin, remove fat and place trimmed ham in baking dish.

- When ready to bake, preheat oven to 275°.

- Combine brown sugar and Worcestershire sauce in bowl. Cut pineapple into halves, forming crescents. Spread brown sugar mixture over ham and place pineapple halves in rows over brown sugar. Pierce each slice with cloves. Bake for 20 minutes or until sugar glaze is brown. Serves 6 to 10.

Old-Fashioned Country Ham

Country ham, any size
1 cup packed brown sugar
2 tablespoons hot mustard
Cola
Whole cloves

- Prepare recipe 2 days ahead. Soak ham in water overnight and wash with stiff brush. Place in roasting pan with 5 cups boiling water.

- Cover and place in cold oven. Turn oven to 500° for 15 minutes and then turn oven off. Leave ham in oven for 3 hours and DO NOT OPEN DOOR.

- Turn oven to 500° again and cook for 15 minutes and then turn off. Leave ham in oven overnight and do not disturb.

- Next day, cut off fat and score ham in diamond pattern. Combine brown sugar, hot mustard and enough cola to make paste. Spread over ham and place whole cloves in each diamond. Bake at 350° for 30 minutes.

Miss Sadie: *"Some Southerners think country ham is just not complete without red eye gravy. My daddy loved it. He used the drippin's from the salty ham, added a little black coffee and made a thin, but wonderful gravy."*

Saucy Ham Loaf

Make this mustard sauce the day before you make the ham loaf.

Sweet-and-Hot Mustard Sauce:

4 ounces dry mustard
1 cup vinegar
3 eggs, beaten
1 cup sugar

- Combine mustard and vinegar in bowl and mix until smooth. Set aside overnight. Add eggs and sugar and cook in double boiler and stir constantly for 8 to 10 minutes or until mixture coats spoon. Cool and chill in covered jars.

Ham Loaf:

1 pound ground ham
½ pound ground beef
½ pound ground pork
2 eggs
1 cup bread or cracker crumbs
2 teaspoons Worcestershire sauce
1 (5 ounce) can evaporated milk
3 tablespoons chili sauce
1 teaspoon seasoned salt
1 teaspoon seasoned pepper
Bacon strips for top of loaf, optional

- Ask butcher to grind 3 meats together for ham loaf.

- Preheat oven to 350°.

- Combine all loaf ingredients except bacon in bowl. Form into loaf in 9 x 13-inch baking pan. Strip bacon on top and bake for 1 hour. Serves 8 to 10.

Raisin Sauce for Ham

1 cup raisins
¼ cup vinegar
¼ cup packed brown sugar
1 teaspoon mustard
1 teaspoon Worcestershire sauce
1 tablespoon flour
1 tablespoon butter

- Cook raisins in 1 cup water for 10 minutes over medium heat. Remove from heat and set aside.

- Combine remaining ingredients and ½ teaspoon salt in bowl and add to raisins. Cook mixture until thick and add butter, if desired. Yields 2½ cups.

Supreme Ham Casserole

2 cups cooked, cubed ham
1 onion, chopped
1 red bell pepper, seeded, chopped
2 ribs celery, chopped
1 (6 ounce) box white and wild rice mix
1 (4 ounce) jar diced pimientos, drained
1 (8 ounce) package shredded colby cheese
2 (10 ounce) cans cream of chicken soup

- Preheat oven to 350°.

- Combine all ingredients plus amount of water called for on box of rice in bowl. Mix well.

- Spoon mixture into sprayed 9 x 13-inch baking dish. Cover and bake for 1 hour. Serves 8.

Baked Stuffed Striped Bass

¾ cup minced onion
¾ cup finely chopped mushrooms
½ cup minced celery
3 tablespoons oil
1½ - 2 pounds striped bass fillets
1 lemon
2 large tomatoes, thinly sliced

- Preheat oven to 375°.

- Saute onion, mushrooms and celery in skillet with oil until onions are translucent. Add breadcrumbs and a little salt and pepper and mix.

- Spray large baking pan and place striper fillets touching each other. Squeeze a little lemon juice over fillets. Place tomato slices on top and salt and pepper lightly.

- Spread breadcrumb mixture over top. Bake uncovered about 30 minutes or until fillets are opaque and flake easily. Serves 4 to 6.

Baked Rockfish Flounder

2 - 3 pound whole flounder
3 or more strips bacon
4 medium-sized potatoes
2 or more onions
1 (8 ounce) can tomato sauce
1 lemon, cut in wedges
Fresh parsley

- Preheat oven to 325°.

- Salt fish on both sides and cut slits on top. Place in sprayed glass baking dish. With knife blade, press strips of bacon into slits. Bake until fish browns. Remove from oven.

- Steam potatoes and onion until tender and arrange ring of potatoes and onion over baked fish. Pour tomato sauce and enough water over fish to keep it moist. (Use water from onions and potatoes. Make sure water is still warm. Never add cold water to anything you cook). Add pepper, as desired.

- Return dish to oven and bake for 20 minutes or until done. Baste once. Garnish with lemon wedges and parsley before serving. Serves 6 to 8.

The Eastern Shore Seafood Festival in Chincoteague, Virginia is held in May. It is an "All You Can Eat" festival and features steamed little neck clams, oysters-on-the-half-shell, clam chowder, fried clams and fried fish, shrimp Creole, chicken tenders, French-fried sweet potatoes, coleslaw and hush puppies.

Seaside Red Snapper

1 (3 - 5 pound) whole butterflied red snapper
½ cup (1 stick) butter, melted
Flour
Sea salt
Cracked black pepper
Fresh dill weed
3 - 4 tablespoons white wine
1 cucumber, sliced
Paprika

- Preheat oven to 350°.

- Rinse and pat dry inside and outside of red snapper. Brush melted butter on inside and outside of snapper, but set aside some for later.

- Sprinkle flour, sea salt and black pepper on inside and outside of snapper thoroughly. Place fresh dill weed inside fish and close.

- Pour white wine in sprayed baking dish. Carefully lay snapper in dish and bake for 20 minutes. Remove dish from oven, baste with set aside butter and add a little more white wine, if needed.

- Return to oven and bake for additional 20 to 25 minutes or until fish flakes. Remove dill weed. Carefully place whole snapper on serving plate and garnish with cucumber slices and dashes of paprika. Serves 8.

Low Country Muddle

"Muddle" is a term used by early settlers meaning "a mess of fish".
It's a basic measurement that all Southerners understand.

2 large bell peppers, seeded, chopped
4 ribs celery, chopped
2 onions, chopped
2 cloves garlic, minced
Vegetable oil
6 cups clam juice
10 - 12 clams, cleaned
10 - 12 mussels, cleaned
10 - 12 shrimp
1 - 1½ pounds flounder

- Cook bell peppers, celery, onions and garlic in a little oil in large stockpot until onions are translucent. Pour in clam juice and clams. Cook until clams open. Add mussels, shrimp and flounder. Cook until shrimp turns pink. Serves 8 to 10.

TIP: Throw away any clams or mussels that didn't open.

The annual World Catfish Festival is held in Belzoni, Mississippi which claims the title of Catfish Capital of the World.

Beer-Battered Fried Catfish

*The recipe for Golden-Fried Hush Puppies is
on page 62 and will make this meal complete.*

¾ cup flour
¾ cup cornstarch
2 tablespoons seasoned salt
1 teaspoon cayenne pepper
1 tablespoon garlic powder
1 teaspoon baking powder
1 egg
1 cup beer, room temperature
Vegetable oil
2 pounds catfish fillets

- Mix flour, cornstarch, seasoned salt, cayenne pepper, garlic
  powder and baking powder together in large flat pie pan or
  baking pan.

- Beat egg slightly and stir into mixture. Add beer, stir well
  and refrigerate, covered, for about 2 hours.

- Just before cooking, heat enough oil in large skillet to cover
  all fillets. Stir batter and dredge each fillet in mixture on
  both sides.

- Carefully place battered fillets in hot oil over medium high
  heat and fry several minutes on both sides until golden
  brown. Drain on paper towel and keep warm in oven. Cook
  remaining fillets and serve immediately. Serves about 4 to 6.

Fried Catfish

*The best frying is done in a cast-iron skillet and everybody
in the South knows that. So the best thing you can
do with this recipe is to start with an iron skillet.*

Fresh catfish fillets
Cracker crumbs or cornmeal
Canola oil

- Wash fillets and pat dry with paper towels. Pour cracker crumbs or cornmeal in shallow bowl and add a little salt and pepper. Dredge fillets in crumbs and coat well.

- Pour enough oil in skillet to cover fish about halfway. When oil is very hot, carefully place fillets one at a time em in skillet. When fish is crispy and golden brown on 1 side, turn and cook until crispy and golden brown on other side. Serve hot.

Hamphreys County, Mississippi is considered to be the Catfish Capital of the World.

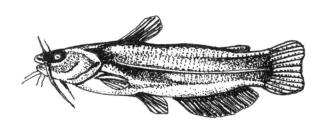

Crisp Oven-Fried Fish

¼ cup milk
1 egg, beaten
1 cup corn flake crumbs
¼ teaspoon thyme
¼ cup parmesan cheese
2 pounds fish fillets
⅓ cup (⅔ stick) butter, melted
Fresh parsley
Lemon slices or wedges

- Preheat oven to 425°.

- Combine milk and egg in shallow dish.

- In separate shallow dish, combine corn flake crumbs, thyme and cheese.

- Dip fillets in milk-egg mixture, roll in crumb-cheese mixture and place side-by-side in sprayed baking dish. Set aside leftover crumb-cheese mixture. Drizzle with melted butter.

- Pour remaining crumb-cheese mixture over top and bake for 12 to 15 minutes. Serve with parsley and lemon. Serves 6 to 8.

Shrimp-Asparagus Casserole

¼ cup (½ stick) butter, divided
24 saltine crackers, coarsely crumbled, divided
2 (15 ounce) cans green asparagus spears, drained
4 eggs, hard-boiled, sliced
1½ pounds shrimp, boiled, chopped coarsely
1 (10 ounce) can cream of mushroom soup
¾ cup milk
1 tablespoon onion juice
1 (8 ounce) package shredded cheddar cheese

- Preheat oven to 325°.

- Grease a 9 x 13-inch baking dish liberally with butter.
  Place half cracker crumbs in baking dish. Layer asparagus,
  eggs and shrimp. Lightly salt and pepper each layer as you
  build casserole.

- Combine soup, milk and onion juice in bowl and pour over
  casserole mixture. Sprinkle top with cheese and remaining
  crumbs, dot with remaining butter and bake for 20 minutes.
  Serves 8.

Shrimp Mousse

Easy! Prepare a day ahead and store in refrigerator.
Use as appetizer, salad or main dish.

1 (10 ounce) can tomato soup
1½ tablespoons unflavored gelatin
2 (3 ounce) packages cream cheese, softened
1 cup mayonnaise
1 tablespoon horseradish
1 tablespoon Worcestershire sauce
2 cups cooked, finely chopped shrimp
1 cup finely chopped celery
⅓ cup chopped fresh or frozen onions

- Heat soup to a boil in saucepan.

- Soften gelatin in ½ cup cold water in large bowl. Pour hot soup over gelatin and stir until it dissolves.

- Beat in cream cheese, mayonnaise, horseradish, Worcestershire sauce and ½ teaspoon salt. Stir in shrimp, celery, and onions and pour mixture into 1½-quart mold. Chill until firm overnight or for 24 hours. Unmold on platter. Serves 8 to 10.

TIP: *Mold into square baking dish and cut into separate servings*
for luncheon or dinner entree. Serve on lettuce
leaves with green vegetable and lemon tart.

Low Country Shrimp Boil

2 pounds kielbasa or link sausage, cut in bite-size pieces
8 large ears corn-on-the cob, halved
14 - 16 new (red) potatoes with peels
2 onions
Shrimp boil or Old Bay® crab boil
4 - 5 pounds shrimp in shells

- Place sausage, corn-on-the-cob, potatoes, onions,
  1 to 2 tablespoons salt, shrimp boil and enough water
  to cover in large stockpot. Bring to a boil and cook
  for 15 to 20 minutes or until potatoes are almost tender.

- Add shrimp and cook for additional 5 minutes or until
  shrimp turn pink. Drain and serve. Serves 10 to 12.

   The Low Country of South Carolina the coastal
plain of the state. First settled more than 300 years
ago by English settlers and slaves from Barbados,
the area is rich in history and local traditions. Rice
brought great wealth to planters and hard work for the
African-Americans who supplied the labor.

   Many of the traditional dishes from the region include rice,
shrimp, crab, oysters, fried okra and fried chicken, just to name
a few.

Fried Shrimp

Have a little patience with these and you'll be well rewarded.

Fresh shrimp
Lemons
Cayenne pepper
Flour
Eggs, beaten
Cracker crumbs or cornmeal
Canola oil

- Wash shrimp, remove veins and shells (except for last segment), but keep tails. Spread tails and press down with large spoon. Squeeze fresh lemon juice generously over shrimp. Sprinkle cayenne pepper lightly over shrimp and marinate shrimp in refrigerator for 30 minutes.

- Mix flour with salt and pepper in shallow bowl. Dredge shrimp through flour and coat generously. Set aside for 30 minutes.

- Dip shrimp in beaten egg and dredge in cracker crumbs. Deep-fry shrimp in very hot oil, carefully adding shrimp one at a time. When shrimp is crispy and golden brown, remove from oil and drain well.

The unusual ecosystem of South Carolina's Low Country provides habitat for alligator, blue heron, egret, anhinga, bald eagle and migratory waterfowl.

Favorite Salmon Croquettes

*What shape are your croquettes? Are they round
logs, flat patties or triangular-shaped logs? No
matter how you shape them, these are great!*

1 (15 ounce) can salmon
½ teaspoon seasoned salt
¼ cup shrimp cocktail sauce or chili sauce
1 (10 ounce) can cream of chicken soup, divided
1 egg
½ onion, finely chopped
Several dashes hot sauce
1⅓ cups cracker crumbs
Flour
Vegetable oil

- Drain salmon well in colander and remove skin and bones.

- Combine salmon, seasoned salt, ½ teaspoon pepper, cocktail
  sauce, half soup, egg, onion, hot sauce and cracker crumbs in
  bowl and mix well.

- Pat mixture into logs with 3 sides about 3 inches long and
  roll in flour. Make about 10 to 12 logs.

- Pour just enough oil in large skillet to cover bottom. Turn
  to medium heat, place croquettes in skillet and fry. Turn
  twice so you have 3 sides that brown. (Add extra oil halfway
  through cooking if needed.)

- It will take about 15 minutes to fry on 3 sides. (Of course
  you could deep-fry croquettes if you want.) Serves 6 to 8.

TIP: *Use remaining cream of chicken soup by diluting with equal
amount of milk and have a cup of soup as an appetizer.*

Salmon Patties

1 (15 ounce) can salmon, flaked
1 tablespoon mustard
2 eggs, beaten
½ cup milk
1 tablespoon flour
Soda cracker crumbs (about 4 crackers)
Corn oil
Lemon wedges

• In bowl, combine salmon, ¼ teaspoon pepper and mustard and mix well. In heavy pan, mix eggs, milk and flour and cook slowly. Stir constantly until thick. Add salmon mixture and cracker crumbs. Cool and form into patties.

• Heat oil in skillet and fry patties on both sides until brown. Serve with lemon wedges. Serves 6 to 8.

The annual *"Lowcountry Shrimp Festival and Blessing of the Fleet"* is held in May in McClellanville, South Carolina.

Savannah-Style Deviled Crabs

Delicious for brunch, lunch or supper – make
in advance and chill until baking time.

½ pound crabmeat
½ cup cracker crumbs
1½ tablespoons butter, melted
1 egg, hard-boiled, diced
1 tablespoon Worcestershire sauce
2 tablespoons dry sherry or dry white wine
¼ teaspoon hot sauce
¼ cup plus 1 tablespoon mayonnaise, divided
1 tablespoon dijon-style mustard
¼ teaspoon ground nutmeg
4 clean crab shells
¼ teaspoon paprika

- Preheat oven to 350°.

- Carefully pick over crabmeat for bits of shell. Toss crumbs in butter in bowl. Add ¼ teaspoon salt and remaining ingredients except 1 tablespoon mayonnaise, crab shells and paprika. Mix well and pile into crab shells.

- "Frost" top of each mound with remaining mayonnaise and dust with paprika. Bake for 15 minutes and place under broiler for 1 to 2 minutes or until mayonnaise topping puffs and browns slightly. Serves 4.

Seacoast Crab Devils

2 tablespoons butter
3 tablespoons flour
1 cup chicken broth
⅓ cup whipping cream
⅛ teaspoon cayenne pepper
2 egg yolks
1 (4 ounce) can sliced mushrooms
1 tablespoon dried parsley
2 (6 ounce) cans crabmeat, well-drained, flaked
6 crab shells or ramekins
⅓ cup seasoned breadcrumbs

- Preheat oven to 350°.

- Melt butter in skillet over medium heat. Slowly mix in flour, broth and cream and stir well. Add ½ teaspoon salt, cayenne pepper and egg yolks and continue to stir and cook until thick. Add mushrooms, parsley and crabmeat to mixture and blend well.

- Pour into lightly buttered shells or ramekins. Cover with breadcrumbs and bake for 10 minutes or until light brown. Serves 6.

The annual Savannah Seafood Festival is held in the fall in Savannah, Georgia.

Crab Delight

2 tablespoons chopped green bell pepper
2 tablespoons butter
2 tablespoons flour
Dash cayenne pepper
½ teaspoon mustard
½ teaspoon Worcestershire sauce
1 cup chopped tomatoes, drained
1 cup shredded cheddar cheese
1 egg, slightly beaten
1⅔ cups scalded milk
1 cup flaked crabmeat
6 patty shells or toasted rounds

- Brown bell pepper in butter in saucepan and add flour and mix until smooth.

- Combine cayenne pepper, mustard, Worcestershire sauce, ¼ teaspoon salt, tomatoes, cheese and egg in bowl and add to bell pepper mixture.

- Cook mixture in double boiler for 10 minutes. Stir constantly and add milk slowly. Add crabmeat and heat thoroughly. Serve on patty shells or toast rounds. Serves 6.

Betty Jo's Crab Cakes

1 pound crabmeat
1 large egg, lightly beaten
2 tablespoons minced onion
2 tablespoons mayonnaise
1 tablespoon Worcestershire sauce
1 tablespoon mustard
½ - ¾ teaspoons hot sauce
¾ cup buttery cracker crumbs
Vegetable oil

- Combine 1 teaspoon salt, ½ teaspoon pepper and remaining ingredients except cracker crumbs and oil in bowl and mix well.

- Place cracker crumbs in shallow bowl. Shape crab mixture into 6 patties and roll in cracker crumbs.

- Fry in skillet for about 3 minutes on each side. Drain. Serves 6.

Miss Sadie: *"Now, the best crab cakes I ever had were in Maryland. They were just some kind o' good."*

Mary Beth's Crab Casserole

1 pound fresh mushrooms
Butter
2 pounds crabmeat
2 cups mayonnaise
1 (1 pint) carton whipping cream
2 tablespoons chopped onion
2 tablespoons parsley
4 eggs, hard-boiled, diced
1 (8 ounce) package herb stuffing mix

- Preheat oven to 350°.

- Slice and saute mushrooms in butter in skillet. Mix with remaining ingredients in bowl, but save a little stuffing to be used for topping.

- Pour in sprayed 9 x 13-inch pan and top with remaining stuffing mix. Bake for 40 minutes. Serves 8 to 10.

Aunt Edna's Crabmeat Casserole

This is just as easy as can be.

½ cup chopped celery
½ cup chopped green bell pepper
¼ cup chopped onion
Butter
1 pound crabmeat
3 - 4 eggs, hard-boiled, chopped
1½ cups seasoned breadcrumbs
1 cup mayonnaise
1 tablespoon dry mustard
1 tablespoon vinegar
1 tablespoon lemon juice
1 tablespoon dry horseradish
½ cup white wine
½ cup buttered breadcrumbs
Paprika

- Preheat oven to 350°.

- Saute celery, green pepper and onion with butter in skillet until tender but not brown.

- Combine all ingredients except buttered breadcrumbs and paprika in sprayed 1½-quart baking dish.

- Top with buttered breadcrumbs and sprinkle with paprika. Bake for 20 minutes or until it is thoroughly hot. Serves 6 to 8.

Elegant Luncheon Crab Quiche

Easy!

1 cup shredded Swiss cheese
1 (9 inch) refrigerated piecrust
5 eggs
1½ cups milk or half-and-half cream
½ cup sliced mushrooms
1 (6 ounce) can crabmeat

- Preheat oven to 375°.

- Sprinkle cheese into piecrust. Beat eggs in bowl and mix with milk, ½ teaspoon and ⅛ teaspoon pepper.

- Pour over cheese in piecrust and sprinkle with mushrooms and crabmeat. Bake for 35 to 55 minutes until firm. Serves 6.

Miss Sadie: "*I just love ladies' luncheons, especially now that hats are back.*"

King Crab Casserole

1 (10 ounce) package frozen broccoli spears or asparagus
½ cup shredded sharp cheddar cheese
6 tablespoons (¾ stick) butter, divided
2 tablespoons minced onion
2 tablespoons flour
¼ teaspoon curry powder
1 cup milk
1 tablespoon lemon juice
1 (6 ounce) package frozen king crab, thawed, drained
2 slices bread

- Preheat oven to 350°.

- Cook broccoli or asparagus according to package directions and drain. Arrange in sprayed 8 x 8-inch baking dish and sprinkle cheese over top.

- Melt ¼ cup butter in saucepan, add onions and saute until soft. Add flour, curry powder, ½ teaspoon salt and milk and stir constantly until thick. Stir in lemon juice and crab. Pour heated mixture over broccoli or asparagus.

- Spread 2 tablespoons butter over bread and cut into cubes. Sprinkle over crab mixture and bake for 30 minutes. Serves 8.

Hard-Shell Blue Crabs

Blue crabs are the most popular Atlantic crab.

8 - 10 live hard-shell blue crabs
Butter or cocktail sauce

- Boil 2 quarts water in soup pot and drop crabs in pot. Cover and boil for 10 minutes; lower heat and cook for additional 10 minutes. Remove with tongs and drain.

- Remove tail flap on underneath side of crab. Remove hard shell on top. Remove legs and white gills on both sides of body. Discard all shells, gills and internal organs.

- Use nutcracker to remove meat from legs and claws. Use small cocktail fork to remove meat from body. Break body in 2 pieces to reach all meat inside cavities. Serve with melted butter and/or cocktail sauce. Serves 6.

Scalloped Oysters

½ cup (1 stick) butter
1 cup cracker crumbs
½ cup seasoned breadcrumbs
1 pint oysters, drained, set aside liquor
2 tablespoons light cream, divided

- Preheat oven to 400°.

- Melt butter in saucepan and pour into small bowl with cracker crumbs and breadcrumbs. Toss mixture to coat well.

- Place one-third crumb mixture in sprayed shallow baking dish and cover with half oysters. Sprinkle with salt and pepper.

- Add 1 tablespoon of oyster liquor to mixture and 1 tablespoon light cream. Repeat process for second layer, top with remaining crumb mixture and bake for 30 minutes. Serves 6.

Miss Sadie: *"Honey, now don't you forget to say 'thank you'; 'no, sir'; and 'yes, ma'am'. It shows respect, especially for your elders.",*

Fried Oysters

Measurements just don't work with this recipe,
so just make sure you have enough of everything.

Fresh oysters, shucked
Cracker crumbs or cornmeal
Canola oil

- Wash and pat dry oysters. Pour cracker crumbs or cornmeal in shallow bowl and add a little salt and pepper. Roll oysters in crumbs and coat well.

- Heat oil in deep fryer. When oil is very hot, carefully add oysters one at a time and place them so they do not touch. When oysters are crispy and golden brown, remove from oil and drain. Serve hot.

Tartar Sauce

⅓ cup sweet pickle relish, drained
2 tablespoons minced onion
1½ cups mayonnaise

- Combine all ingredients in bowl and mix well. Yields 2 cups.

Smothered Quail, Southern Style

6 - 8 cleaned quail
Flour
½ cup (1 stick) butter
1½ cups milk
Cooked rice or biscuits

- Salt and pepper quail and roll in flour. Melt butter in very large skillet, cover and brown quail over medium heat. Turn quail several times. Remove quail and set aside.

- Add 3 tablespoons flour and a little more salt and pepper to skillet and lightly brown flour over low heat. Slowly stir in and cook enough milk to make white gravy.

- Return quail to skillet, roll in gravy and cover. Simmer over low heat for 45 minutes and baste every 15 minutes. Serve gravy over rice or biscuits. Serves 6 to 8.

Georgia is often recognized as the "Quail Capital of the World" and hunters come from around the world. Two-thirds of the quail population can be harvested with no reduction in the spring breeding population.

Billy Earl's Stewed Goose

Billy Earl's goose is stewed.

1 goose, cleaned, cut up, parboiled
2 tablespoons vegetable oil
Flour dumplings (recipe below)

- Place prepared fowl in large heavy pot, cover with 2 quarts water and oil and bring to a boil. Reduce heat and simmer for 2 hours or until tender.

- Turn heat up, bring to boil again and drop dumplings by heaping tablespoonfuls into pot. Boil for about 10 minutes. Reduce heat and simmer for 1 hour and stir occasionally to prevent burning. Serves 4 to 6.

Flour Dumplings:

1 cup flour
2 teaspoons baking powder
½ cup milk
2 tablespoons vegetable oil

- Sift flour, baking powder and ½ teaspoon salt in bowl.

- In separate bowl, combine milk and oil and add to dry ingredients. Stir until mixture is just moist. Batter will be lumpy.

Barbecued Duck Breasts

1 (10 ounce) can cream of onion soup
½ cup ketchup
¼ cup (½ stick) butter
4 drops hot sauce
2 cloves garlic, minced
2 ribs celery, sliced
1 green bell pepper, seeded, finely chopped
4 wild duck breasts
8 slices bacon

- Combine soup, ketchup, butter, hot sauce, garlic, ¼ teaspoon each of salt and pepper, celery, bell pepper, and ½ cup water. Bring mixture to a boil, reduce heat and simmer for 30 minutes. Cool.

- Remove each breast half from duck as intact as possible and remove skin. Wrap each breast half with slice of bacon and secure with toothpick. Cover breasts with sauce and marinate for 3 hours in refrigerator.

- Grill over hot coals for 3 to 4 minutes on each side. Cook remaining marinade for gravy. Serves 6.

Waterfowl along the Mississippi Flyway, whitetail deer, wild turkey and small game are plentiful in Arkansas.

Arkansas is known as the Duck Hunting Capital of the World.

Heavenly Dove

6 doves, dressed
Flour
2 tablespoons butter
⅛ teaspoon thyme
⅛ teaspoon rosemary
1 teaspoon finely chopped parsley
1 medium onion, finely chopped
1 (4 ounce) can mushrooms with liquid
1 cup sauterne wine
Wild rice or rice, cooked

- Cut doves along backbone and butterfly by removing large bones of lower back and legs. Press flat and roll in flour. Brown lightly in butter in skillet and sprinkle with herbs and parsley.

- Cover and cook slowly for 15 minutes. Add onions, mushrooms with liquid and wine.

- Cover and simmer for 1 hour or until tender. Add ½ teaspoon salt 5 minutes before removing from heat. Serve with wild rice or rice. Serves 6.

TIP: Quail or squab may be substituted for doves.

Kentucky has more than one million acres designated as national parks and recreational areas. The Daniel Boone National Park, Mammoth Cave National Park, Cumberland Gap National Historical Park, the Big South Fork National River and Recreation Area and the Land Between the Lakes include rivers, streams, mountains, lush forests, ancient caves and natural attractions that are some of the most beautiful scenery in the world.

Joe David's Roast Venison

4 pounds venison roast
1 (1 ounce) packet onion soup mix
¼ cup vinegar
1 tablespoon soy sauce
1 tablespoon Worcestershire sauce
1 large onion, sliced
1 piece suet

- Preheat oven to 325°.

- Wash and trim meat. Soak overnight in salted water to cover. Drain off water and resoak in fresh salted water for 1 hour. Trim off shreds of whitish membranes.

- Sprinkle soup mix into baking pan and add roast.

- Combine vinegar, soy sauce and Worcestershire sauce in bowl and spoon over meat. Place onion slices on top of meat. Cut strips of suet and secure to meat with toothpicks.

- Cover pan with foil and seal edges around lip of pan and bake for 4 hours. Serves 6 to 8.

The Mississippi Sandhill Crane is about 44 inches tall and has an eight-foot wingspan. It is the rarest of North American cranes with a population of only a little over 100 birds. It can be found in the grassy savannas in and around the Mississippi Sandhill Crane National Wildlife Refuge in Jackson County, Mississippi.

Dandy, Delicious Desserts

Miss Sadie's Oven-Fresh Cakes

Dreamin' Steamin' Pies

Mama's Homemade Cookies

Delicious Daily Desserts

Sweet, Sweet Candies

Apricot Nectar Cake

The longer this sits, the better it tastes.

Cake:

1 (18 ounce) box lemon cake mix
1 cup apricot nectar
4 eggs
¾ cup vegetable oil
½ cup sugar

• Preheat oven to 350°.

• Combine all ingredients in bowl and mix well. Bake in
  sprayed, floured tube pan for 1 hour. Cool for 5 minutes,
  remove from pan and glaze while hot.

Glaze:

Juice from 1 lemon
1½ cups powdered sugar

• Combine ingredients in bowl and pour slowly over hot cake
  so glaze seeps into cake. Spread remaining glaze on sides of
  cake. Serves 18 to 20.

TIP: *Make recipe the day before you eat so icing has time to seep
     into cake. It's wonderful and will store just fine.*

Lumberton, Mississippi is the home of the world's
largest pecan nursery.

Carrot Cake

2 cups sifted flour
2 cups sugar
1 teaspoon baking powder
1 teaspoon baking soda
1 teaspoon ground cinnamon
4 eggs
1½ cups vegetable oil
2 cups grated carrots

- Preheat oven to 350°.

- Sift ¼ teaspoon salt and dry ingredients in bowl.

- In separate bowl, combine eggs and oil. Add dry ingredients and mix thoroughly. Stir in carrots. Pour into 3 sprayed, floured 9-inch layer cake pans and bake for 30 to 40 minutes.

Frosting:

1 (8 ounce) package cream cheese, softened
½ cup (1 stick) butter
1 teaspoon vanilla
1 (16 ounce) package powdered sugar
1 cup chopped pecans

- Beat cream cheese and butter in bowl. Add vanilla and powdered sugar. Frost cake and sprinkle with pecans. Serves 18 to 20.

The RC® and MoonPie® Festival is held annually in Bell Buckle, Tennessee. RC cola with a MoonPie is a true Southern tradition.

Strawberry Cake

1 (18 ounce) box white cake mix
1 tablespoon flour
1 (3 ounce) box strawberry gelatin
1 (10 ounce) package frozen strawberries, thawed, divided
1 cup corn oil
4 eggs

- Preheat oven to 350°.

- Spray and flour 2 (8 or 9 inch) layer pans or spray and flour sides of pans and cut out circle of wax paper to fit bottom of pan.

- Combine cake mix, flour and gelatin in bowl and mix well.

- In separate bowl, mix ¾ cup strawberries, ½ cup water and corn oil. Add to cake mixture and blend well.

- Add eggs one at a time and beat for 1 minute after each egg. Pour into pans and bake for 35 minutes.

Frosting:

½ cup (1 stick) butter
2½ - 3 cups powdered sugar
2 tablespoons milk

- Cream butter and sugar with milk in bowl. Add small amount of remaining strawberries for color. If frosting is too thin, add more powdered sugar. Frost cake and chill for several hours before serving. Serves 18-20.

Fresh Apple Cake

1½ cups vegetable oil
2½ cups sugar
1 teaspoon vanilla
3 eggs
3 cups flour
1 teaspoon baking soda
1 tablespoon ground cinnamon
3 cups apples, peeled, cored, chopped
1 cup chopped nuts

- Preheat oven to350°.

- Combine oil, sugar and vanilla in bowl until smooth and creamy. Add eggs and mix well.

- Sift in flour, baking soda and cinnamon. (Batter will be stiff.) Add apples and nuts to mixture and beat thoroughly.

- Pour into sprayed, floured tube pan. Bake for 1 hour 30 minutes. Serves 18.

Rummy Yum Cake

Cake:

1 cup chopped pecans or walnuts
1 (18 ounce) box yellow cake mix
½ cup dark rum
1 (3 ounce) package vanilla instant pudding mix
4 eggs, beaten
½ cup vegetable oil

- Preheat oven to 325°.

- Sprinkle nuts in sprayed, floured 10-inch tube or 12-cup bundt pan.

- Combine ½ cup cold water and remaining ingredients in bowl and pour over nuts and bake for 1 hour. Cool. Invert cake on serving plate.

Glaze:

½ cup (1 stick) butter
1 cup sugar
½ cup dark rum

- Melt butter in saucepan and stir in ¼ cup water and sugar. Boil for 5 minutes and stir constantly. Remove from heat and add rum. Prick top of cake and drizzle glaze evenly over top and sides. Allow cake to absorb glaze and repeat until glaze is completely used. Serves 18 to 20.

Lemon Cake

Cake:

1 (18 ounce) box yellow cake mix
4 eggs
1 (3 ounce) package lemon gelatin
¾ cup vegetable oil

• Preheat oven to 350°.

• Combine all ingredients with ¾ cup water in bowl and beat until fluffy. Pour into sprayed, floured 9 x 13-inch baking pan. Bake for 30 to 35 minutes.

• Remove cake from oven and jab with fork to bottom at 1-inch intervals.

Glaze:

2 cups powdered sugar
1 teaspoon grated lemon peel
Juice of 2 lemons
1 (7 ounce) package flaked coconut

• Combine powdered sugar, lemon peel and juice in bowl.

• Spoon glaze mixture over warm cake, sprinkle with coconut and serve warm. Serves 16 to 18.

Lemon-Pecan Holiday Cake

1 (1.5 ounce) bottle lemon extract
4 cups pecan halves
2 cups (4 sticks) butter
3 cups sugar
3½ cups flour, divided
1½ teaspoons baking powder
6 eggs
½ pound candied green pineapple, chopped
½ pound candied red cherries, halved

- Preheat oven to 275°.

- Pour lemon extract over pecans in medium bowl, toss and set aside.

- Cream butter and sugar in large bowl until fluffy.

- In separate bowl, sift 3 cups flour and baking powder. Add eggs to butter-sugar mixture, one at a time, alternating with flour mixture.

- Place pineapple and cherries in separate bowl, add ½ cup flour and mix until flour covers fruit well. Fold fruit and pecans into batter and pour in sprayed, floured tube cake pan.

- Bake for 2 hours 30 minutes to 2 hours 45 minutes. Cake is done when toothpick inserted in center comes out clean. Cool and remove carefully from pan. Serves 20.

Pecans contain no cholesterol and add essential fiber, vitamin E, magnesium, thiamin and copper to the diet. They are also high in monounsaturated fats that help lower LDL cholesterol blood levels.

Mississippi Mud Cake

2 cups sugar
⅓ cup cocoa
1½ cups (3 sticks) butter
4 eggs
1 teaspoon vanilla
1½ cups flour
1⅓ cups flaked coconut
1½ cups chopped pecans
1 (7 ounce) jar marshmallow creme

- Preheat oven to 350°.

- Cream sugar, cocoa, and butter in bowl and add eggs and vanilla. Mix well. Stir in flour, coconut, and pecans.

- Pour into sprayed 9 x 13-inch baking pan and bake for 40 minutes. When done, spread marshmallow creme over hot cake. Cool before frosting.

Frosting:

1 (1 pound) box powdered sugar
⅓ cup cocoa
½ cup (1 stick) butter, softened
½ cup evaporated milk
1 teaspoon vanilla

- Sift together powdered sugar and cocoa in bowl. Cream butter with dry ingredients, then stir in evaporated milk and vanilla. Spread over cake. Serves 16 to 18.

Chocolate Picnic Cake

Cake:

2 cups flour
2 cups sugar
½ cup (1 stick) butter
½ cup shortening
5 tablespoons cocoa
½ cup buttermilk*
2 eggs
1 teaspoon baking soda
1 teaspoon vanilla

- Preheat oven to 350°.

- Sift flour and sugar in bowl. Combine 1 cup water, butter, shortening and cocoa in saucepan and heat until they melt. Cool, pour over flour-sugar mixture and mix well.

- Add buttermilk, eggs, baking soda and vanilla and mix well. Pour into sprayed 9 x 13-inch baking pan and bake for 25 to 35 minutes.

Frosting:

½ cup (1 stick) butter
6 tablespoons milk
¼ cup cocoa
1 (1 pound) box powdered sugar
1 teaspoon vanilla
Chopped nuts

- Bring butter, milk and cocoa in saucepan to a boil. Remove from heat and add powdered sugar, vanilla and nuts. Pour over hot cake. Serves 16 to 18.

TIP: To make buttermilk, mix 1 cup milk with 1 tablespoon lemon juice or vinegar and let milk stand for about 10 minutes.

Sour Cream-Chocolate Chip Cake

This is so easy!

1 cup (2 sticks) butter
1¼ cups sugar
3 eggs, lightly beaten
1 (8 ounce) carton sour cream
2 cups cake flour
½ teaspoon baking soda
1 teaspoon baking powder
1 teaspoon vanilla
1 (12 ounce) package miniature chocolate chips
1 cup chopped pecans

- Preheat oven to 350°.

- Cream butter and sugar in bowl until smooth. Add eggs and sour cream and mix well.

- Sift together cake flour, baking soda and baking powder and stir into mixture. Add vanilla, chocolate chips and pecans.

- Pour into sprayed tube pan and bake for 1 hour. Serves 18.

Although the origin of angel food cake is a little fuzzy, similar cakes appeared in Mrs. Porter's New Southern Cookery Book and Companion for Frugal and Economical Housekeepers in 1871 and in What Mrs. Fisher Knows About Old Southern Cooking, Soups, Pickles, Preserves, Etc. in 1881. Abbey Fisher, a former Alabama slave, recorded a recipe for Silver Cake, thought to be the source of angel food cake. A reason the South is considered as the origin is because strong African-American slaves probably did the hand beating required for the recipe. The cake was also a favorite to serve by African-Americans.

Ashley Baine's Chess Cake

Crust:

1 (18 ounce) box yellow or chocolate cake mix
½ cup (1 stick) butter, softened
1 egg

- Preheat oven to 350°.

- Crumble cake mix in bowl and stir in butter and egg. Pat into sprayed 9 x 13-inch baking pan.

Filling:

1 (8 ounce) package cream cheese, softened
1 (1 pound) box powdered sugar
2 eggs
3 - 4 tablespoons lemon juice for yellow cake or brewed coffee
    for chocolate cake

- Beat cream cheese, powdered sugar, eggs, and lemon juice or coffee in bowl. Blend thoroughly and pour mixture over crust.

- Bake for 35 to 40 minutes or until brown. Serves 16 to 18.

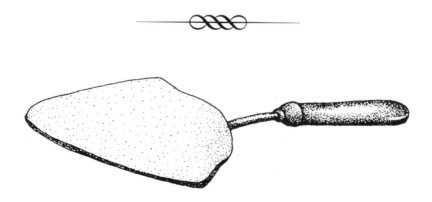

Hummingbird Cake

3 cups flour
2 cups sugar
1 teaspoon ground cinnamon
1 teaspoon baking soda
3 eggs
1½ cups vegetable oil
3 cups mashed bananas
3 cups chopped pecans
1 (8 ounce) can crushed pineapple with juice

- Preheat oven to 325°.

- Sift flour, sugar, 1 teaspoon salt, cinnamon and baking soda in bowl. Add eggs and oil and mix well.

- Fold in bananas, pecans and pineapple. Bake in sprayed large tube pan for 1 hour 15 minutes. Cool and frost.

TIP: An alternate method is to bake in 3 (8 or 9 inch) pans at 350° for 25 to 30 minutes.

Frosting:

½ cup (1 stick) butter, softened
1 (8 ounce) package cream cheese, softened
1 (1 pound) box powdered sugar
1 teaspoon vanilla
1 cup chopped nuts

- Combine butter and cream cheese in bowl and beat until smooth. Add powdered sugar, vanilla and nuts. Spread over layers, top and sides of cooled cake. Serves 18 to 20.

Out-of-This-World Cake

2 cups sugar
1 cup (2 sticks) butter, softened
5 eggs
1 cup milk
1 (13.5 ounce) box graham cracker crumbs
1 tablespoon baking powder
1 (15 ounce) can crushed pineapple, drained
1 (6 ounce) package frozen flaked coconut, thawed
1½ cups chopped nuts
1 tablespoon vanilla

- Preheat oven to 350°.

- Combine all ingredients in bowl and mix well using electric mixer.

- Pour into sprayed, floured tube pan and bake for about 1 hour 20 minutes or when toothpick inserted in center comes out clean. Cool before removing from pan. Serves 18.

Miss Sadie: *"I always bake a cake to take to the family when someone passes away. I have friends who take casseroles, but I've always been partial to cakes."*

Poppy Seed Cake

3 cups sugar
1¼ cups shortening
6 eggs
3 cups flour
¼ teaspoon baking soda
1 cup buttermilk*
3 tablespoons poppy seeds
2 teaspoons almond extract
2 teaspoons vanilla
2 teaspoons butter flavoring

- Preheat oven to 325°.

- Cream sugar and shortening in bowl until mixture is light and fluffy. Add eggs, one at a time, and blend mixture well.

- In separate bowl, sift flour, baking soda and ½ teaspoon salt.

- Alternately add dry ingredients and buttermilk to sugar mixture. Add poppy seeds and flavorings and blend well. Pour into sprayed, floured bundt pan.

- Bake for about 1 hour 15 minutes. Cake is done when toothpick inserted in center comes out clean.

Glaze:

1½ cups powdered sugar
⅓ cup lemon juice
1 teaspoon vanilla
1 teaspoon almond extract

- Combine all ingredients in bowl and mix well. Pour over top of cooled cake and let some glaze run down sides of cake. Serves 20.

TIP: To make buttermilk, mix 1 cup milk with 1 tablespoon lemon juice or vinegar and let milk stand for about 10 minutes.

Festive Christmas Cake

This is easy to make and great if you make the day before.

1 (18 ounce) box lemon supreme pound cake mix
1 (12 ounce) package mixed candied fruit, dredged in flour

- Prepare cake batter according to package directions. Fold candied fruit into batter and pour into cake pan. Bake according to package directions. (Some fruit may be set aside for garnish.)

Frosting:

3 tablespoons butter, softened
1 cup powdered sugar
1½ tablespoons sherry
Candied fruit for garnish

- Cream butter and powdered sugar in bowl. Add sherry gradually until frosting is of spreading consistency. Spread over top of cake and garnish with candied fruit. Serves 18 to 20.

TIP: Cut fruit to represent poinsettia, if desired.

The Only Great Pound Cake

½ cup shortening
1 cup (2 sticks) butter
3 cups sugar
5 eggs
3½ cups flour
½ teaspoon baking powder
1 cup milk
1 teaspoon rum flavoring
1 teaspoon coconut flavoring

- Preheat oven to 325°.

- Cream shortening, butter and sugar in bowl, add eggs and beat for 4 minutes.

- In separate bowl, combine flour and baking powder and add dry ingredients and milk alternately to butter mixture. Begin and end with flour. Add rum and coconut flavorings.

- Pour mixture into large sprayed tube pan and bake for 1 hour 35 minutes. Cake is done when toothpick inserted in center comes out clean. (Do not open door during baking.)

Glaze:

1 cup sugar
½ teaspoon almond extract

- Right before cake is done, combine sugar and ⅓ cup water in saucepan and bring to a rolling boil. Remove from heat and add almond extract. While cake is still in pan, pour glaze over cake and set aside for 30 minutes before removing from pan. Serves 18.

Easy Pound Cake

2 cups flour
1 cup (2 sticks) butter, softened
5 eggs
2 cups sugar
½ cup milk
2 teaspoons baking powder
1 teaspoon vanilla

- Preheat oven to 350°.

- Combine all ingredients and mix for 10 minutes on medium speed. Pour into sprayed tube pan and bake for 50 minutes to 1 hour. Cool. Serves 18.

Pound cakes have been in the South long before the first recorded recipes of the 18th century. They were named pound cakes because of the equal weight of each of the ingredients: 1 pound flour, 1 pound butter, 1 pound sugar and 1 pound eggs. In The Virginia Housewife published in 1824, Mary Randolph uses these ingredients and measurements and suggests adding grated lemon peel, nutmeg and brandy. She also suggests baking as a cake or as a pudding in a large mold and boiling it and serving with butter and sugar.

Double Chocolate Pound Cake

1 cup (2 sticks) butter, softened
½ cup shortening
1 (3 ounce) package cream cheese, softened
3 cups sugar
2 teaspoons vanilla
5 large eggs
½ cup cocoa
3 cups flour
1 teaspoon baking powder
1 cup buttermilk*
1 (6 ounce) package chocolate chips
Powdered sugar

- Preheat oven to 325°.

- Beat butter, shortening, cream cheese and sugar in bowl on high speed for 5 minutes. Add vanilla and eggs and beat well.

- In separate bowl, mix cocoa, flour, baking powder and ½ teaspoon salt. Add half dry ingredients to batter, then buttermilk and end with remaining dry ingredients. Beat well after each addition. Fold in chocolate chips.

- Pour into sprayed, floured 10-inch tube pan and bake for 1 hour 30 minutes. Cake is done when toothpick inserted in center comes out clean. Cool cake in pan for 15 minutes; then turn onto cake plate and cool completely. Dust with sifted powdered sugar. Serves 18 to 20.

TIP: To make buttermilk, mix 1 cup milk with 1 tablespoon lemon juice or vinegar and let milk stand for about 10 minutes.

Praline Cheesecake

1¼ cups graham cracker crumbs
¼ cup sugar
¼ cup (½ stick) butter, melted
3 (8 ounce) packages cream cheese, softened
1¼ cups packed dark brown sugar
2 tablespoons flour
3 large eggs
2 teaspoons vanilla
½ cup finely chopped pecans
Pecan halves
Maple syrup

- Preheat oven to 350°.

- Combine crumbs, sugar and butter in bowl and press in 9-inch springform pan. Bake for 10 minutes.

- Combine cream cheese, brown sugar and flour in bowl and blend on medium speed. Add eggs, one at a time, and mix well after each addition. Blend in vanilla, stir in pecans and pour mixture over crust. Bake for 50 to 55 minutes.

- Remove from oven and loosen cake from rim of pan. Let cake cool before removing from pan. Chill.

- Place pecan halves around edge of cake (about 1 inch from edge and 1 inch apart) and pour syrup over top.

- When you slice cheesecake, pour 1 tablespoon of syrup over each slice so some will run down sides. Serves 16 to 18.

Sissy's Cream Puff Pie

This recipe gives you the same grandeur of
individual cream puffs without the time.

Crust:

¼ cup shortening
½ cup flour
2 eggs

- Preheat oven to 400°.

- Mix ½ cup boiling water, shortening and ⅛ teaspoon salt in saucepan over heat. Stir in flour all at once. Stir until mixture pulls away from sides and forms into a ball.

- Remove from heat and cool slightly. Beat in eggs, one at a time, until smooth. Spread in sprayed 9-inch pie pan but not onto sides.

- Bake for 50 to 60 minutes. Sides will rise up and curl in slightly. Cool slowly away from drafts.

Filling:

1 (4 ounce) package instant vanilla pudding
1 cup whipped cream
Strawberries
1 cup whipped topping, thawed

- Mix vanilla pudding according to package directions. Fold in whipped cream. Pour cream filling into crust and top with strawberries. Top with additional whipped topping. Serves 8.

Peach Mousse Pie

1 (16 ounce) package frozen peach slices, thawed
1 cup sugar
1 (1 ounce) packet unflavored gelatin
⅛ teaspoon ground nutmeg
A few drops of yellow and red food coloring
¾ (12 ounce) carton whipped topping, thawed
1 (9-inch) ready graham cracker or cookie piecrust
Nectarine slices

- Place peaches in blender and process until smooth. Place in saucepan, bring to a boil and stir constantly. Remove from heat.

- Combine sugar, gelatin and nutmeg in separate bowl and stir into hot puree until sugar and gelatin dissolve.

- Pour gelatin mixture into large bowl. Place in freezer for 20 minutes or until mixture mounds slightly when dropped from spoon. Stir occasionally. Beat mixture on high speed for 5 minutes or until mixture becomes light and fluffy.

- Add coloring, fold in whipped topping and pour into piecrust. Garnish with nectarine slices and chill. Serves 8.

More than 40 varieties of peaches are grown in Georgia and harvested between May and August. Clingstone peaches are great for canning, pickling and eating early in the season, but are not generally used for cooking. Freestone varieties have pits that separate easily from the flesh, making them easy to prepare. Varieties that are firm are best for cooking. And late season varieties are best for jams, jellies and preserves because they have more pectin and natural sugars.

Peach Parfait Pie

1 (9 inch) unbaked piecrust
3½ cups sliced fresh peaches
½ - ¾ cup sugar
1 (3 ounce) package lemon gelatin
1 (1 pint) carton vanilla ice cream, softened
1 (8 ounce) carton whipped topping, thawed

- Bake piecrust according to package directions and cool or use a ready graham cracker crust.

- Sweeten fresh peaches with sugar or substitute 1 (29 ounce) can sliced peaches for fresh peaches. If you use fresh peaches, let stand for 15 minutes after mixing with sugar.

- Drain peaches, fresh or canned, and set aside syrup. Add enough water to syrup in saucepan to make 1 cup. Heat to a boil, add gelatin and stir until it dissolves. Add ½ cup cold water.

- Spoon ice cream into mixture and stir until it melts. Chill until mixture mounds slightly when dropped from spoon. Fold in peaches. Turn into piecrust and chill until firm. Top with whipped topping and additional peaches, if desired. Serves 8.

The Elberta Peach, developed in the 19th century in Georgia, quickly became the most widely planted variety of peach ever introduced. Today the most widely cultivated peach is Elegant Lady.

Pineapple-Coconut Pie

1 (9 inch) refrigerated deep-dish piecrust
½ cup (1 stick) butter, melted
2 cups sugar
4 eggs, slightly beaten
1 (10 ounce) can flaked coconut
1 (8 ounce) can pineapple chunks, slightly drained

- Preheat oven to 350°.

- Mix all ingredients in bowl and pour into piecrust. Bake for
  45 minutes to 1 hour or until golden brown. Serves 8.

*Virginia is the birthplace of eight U.S. presidents,
including George Washington, Thomas Jefferson,
James Madison, James Monroe, William Henry
Harrison, John Tyler, Zachary Taylor and
Woodrow Wilson.*

Miss Sadie: *"If you have good manners and keep a
smile on your face, you'll do just fine in this world."*

Strawberry Pie

1 cup sugar
¼ cup cornstarch
¼ cup strawberry gelatin
1 tablespoon lemon juice
2 cups sliced strawberries
2 (8 - 9 inch) piecrusts or 1 deep-dish crust, baked
Whipped topping, thawed

- Combine sugar, cornstarch, gelatin, lemon juice and 1½ cups water in saucepan, cook until thick and stir occasionally. Cool.

- Place berries in piecrusts and pour thickened mixture on top. Chill for at least 3 hours. Serve with whipped topping and garnish with halved or whole strawberries, if desired. Serves 8.

A native wild strawberry grown on the east coast called Fragaria Virginiana was the start of today's strawberries, now grown primarily in California. Cultivation of the wild Virginia strawberry started sometime in the 1600's by colonists who learned about the fruit from Native Americans.

Company Pumpkin Pie

1 (8 ounce) package cream cheese, softened
¾ cup sugar, divided
½ teaspoon vanilla
3 eggs, divided
1 (9 inch) refrigerated piecrust
1¼ cups canned pumpkin
1 teaspoon ground cinnamon
¼ teaspoon ground ginger
¼ teaspoon ground nutmeg
1 cup evaporated milk

- Preheat oven to 350°.

- Beat cream cheese, ¼ cup sugar and vanilla in bowl until they blend. Add 1 egg and mix well. Spread into piecrust.

- Beat remaining eggs slightly and add remaining ingredients (including remaining ½ cup sugar) with a dash of salt in bowl. Mix well and pour over cream cheese mixture. Bake for 65 minutes. Serves 8.

TIP: *Protect piecrust from excess browning by placing 1-inch strip of foil around edges.*

The Edisto River Canoe and Kayak Trail in South Carolina covers 66 miles of the Edisto River. The river is believed to be North America's longest free flowing blackwater stream. The term "blackwater" describes the water's dark color which derives from the tannic acid produced by the trees and other plants along the river as it flows slowly through marshland and swampy areas.

Fannie's
Pumpkin Cream Pie

1 (8 ounce) package cream cheese, softened
2½ cups powdered sugar, divided
1 (8 ounce) carton whipped topping, thawed
2 (6 ounce) ready butter-flavored piecrusts
¼ cup milk
1 (5 ounce) package instant vanilla pudding
1 (15 ounce) can pumpkin
1 teaspoon ground cinnamon
½ teaspoon ground ginger
¼ teaspoon ground cloves

- Combine cream cheese and 2 cups powdered sugar in bowl and beat until smooth and creamy. Fold in whipped topping and pour half mixture in each piecrust.

- In same bowl, combine milk, instant pudding mix and remaining ½ cup powdered sugar and beat until smooth.

- Fold in pumpkin, cinnamon, ginger and cloves. Spread half pumpkin mixture over each pie. Chill for 3 or 4 hours before serving. Eat one pie and freeze the other. Serves 12.

Macaroon Crunch Pie

½ cup plus 2 tablespoons shredded coconut, divided
1 (9 inch) baked piecrust
3 cups orange sherbet, softened
1½ cups whipping cream
⅓ cup powdered sugar
1 cup crushed crisp macaroon cookies
½ cup chopped pecans

- Preheat oven to 325°.

- Toast ½ cup coconut in shallow pan for 5 to 10 minutes or until light brown. Stir often to keep from burning. Remove from oven and sprinkle toasted coconut into piecrust. Cover with sherbet and place in freezer.

- Beat cream and powdered sugar in bowl until thick. Set aside 1 cup for topping.

- Fold crushed cookies and pecans into remaining cream-sugar mixture. Spoon over sherbet and top with set aside whipping cream-powdered sugar mixture and 2 tablespoons coconut. Freeze for 6 hours. Serves 8.

TIP: *This pie will store and freeze well. Also, substitute your choice of sherbet flavor.*

The Charleston Museum in Charleston, South Carolina is known as the first public museum in the United States. It was founded in 1773 and still operates today.

Peanut Pie

You will need to make this in advance and freeze.

1 (3 ounce) package cream cheese
½ cup peanut butter
1 cup powdered sugar
½ cup milk
1 (8 ounce) carton whipped topping, thawed
1 (6 ounce) ready graham cracker piecrust
¼ cup finely chopped peanuts

• Beat cream cheese, peanut butter, powdered sugar and milk in bowl until smooth. Fold in whipped topping.

• Pour into piecrust and top with peanuts. Freeze. Do not thaw before cutting and serving pie. Serves 6.

George Washington Carver is considered the father of the peanut industry because of his research at Tuskegee Institute in Alabama. He discovered and developed more than 300 uses for peanuts. He also convinced Southern farmers that peanuts could be a cash crop and should be planted as a rotation crop. Agriculture in the South was changed forever.

"Goober", meaning peanut, is a derivative of the Bantu (Africa) word "nguba" and came to the U.S. during the African slave trade.

Willa Mae's Pecan Pie

2 tablespoons flour
3 tablespoons butter, melted
3 eggs, beaten
⅔ cup sugar
1 cup corn syrup
1 teaspoon vanilla
1 cup chopped pecans
1 (9 inch) refrigerated piecrust

- Preheat oven to 350°.

- Combine flour, butter, eggs, sugar, corn syrup and vanilla in bowl and mix well.

- Place pecans in piecrust and pour egg mixture over pecans.

- Bake for 10 minutes, reduce heat to 275° and bake for additional 50 to 55 minutes or until center of pie is firm. Serves 8.

TIP: *Protect piecrust from excess browning by placing 1-inch strip of foil around edges.*

Pecans are extremely popular in the South and are used in appetizers, salads, vegetables, main dishes and desserts. Pecans add flavor, texture and crunch to many Southern favorites.

Southern Whiskey Pie

5 eggs
1¾ cups sugar
1 tablespoon vinegar
¼ cup bourbon
⅓ cup (⅔ stick) butter, melted
1 (9 inch) refrigerated piecrust

- Preheat oven to 325°.

- Beat eggs in bowl until light and gradually add sugar. Stir in vinegar, bourbon and butter and mix well.

- Pour into piecrust and bake for 35 minutes until light brown on top. Serve warm or at room temperature. Serves 6.

TIP: Protect piecrust from excess browning by placing 1-inch strip of foil around edges.

Kentucky is known today as the Bluegrass State. The grass is not really blue; it is green. However, in the spring it produces bluish-purple buds that give the grass a blue cast when seen growing in large fields.

Lemon-Pecan Chess Pie

2¼ cups sugar
2 tablespoons flour
1 tablespoon cornmeal
4 eggs, lightly beaten
2 tablespoons grated lemon peel
¼ cup lemon juice
¾ cup chopped pecans
1 (9 inch) refrigerated piecrust

- Preheat oven to 400°.

- Combine sugar, flour and cornmeal in large bowl and toss lightly. Add eggs, lemon peel and lemon juice and mix until smooth and it blends thoroughly. Add pecans to mixture and pour into piecrust.

- Bake for 10 minutes. Reduce heat to 325° and bake for additional 40 to 45 minutes or until center is not shaky. Serves 6.

TIP: Protect piecrust from excess browning by placing 1-inch strip of foil around edges.

The origin of chess pie is probably English. Settlers who made it a specialty brought it to the South. Today, the South claims to be its true home.

Sunny Lemon Chess Pie

3 tablespoons cornmeal
2 cups sugar
¼ cup (½ stick) plus 1 tablespoon butter, melted
4 eggs, slightly beaten
¼ cup lemon juice
½ teaspoon grated lemon peel
1 (9 inch) refrigerated piecrust

- Preheat oven at 350°.

- Combine cornmeal, sugar, butter, eggs, lemon juice and lemon peel in bowl and mix well. Pour into piecrust and bake for 45 minutes or until center is set and brown on top. Serves 6.

Chess pies are Southern specialties. They are a simple mixture of sugar, butter, eggs and a little flour with variations of flavorings such as lemon, vanilla and chocolate. It's believed that "chess" is a corruption of the word "cheese" because chess pie is much like cheeseless cheesecake.

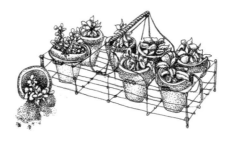

Chocolate Chess Pie

1 (8 - 9 inch) refrigerated piecrust
½ cup (1 stick) butter
1 (1 ounce) square unsweetened chocolate
1 cup sugar
2 eggs
1 teaspoon vanilla
Whipped cream
½ cup nuts

- Preheat oven to 450°.

- If desired, bake crust for about 5 minutes. Remove crust from oven and reduce heat to 350°.

- Melt butter and chocolate in double boiler. Blend in sugar, eggs, vanilla and a dash of salt and thoroughly combine with butter and chocolate.

- Pour into piecrust and bake for 25 to 30 minutes. Cool. Top with whipped cream and nuts. Serves 6.

Chocolate Angel Pie

2 egg whites
⅛ teaspoon cream of tartar
½ cup sugar
½ cup finely chopped walnuts or pecans
1½ teaspoons vanilla, divided
4 (1 ounce) squares German sweet chocolate
1 (8 ounce) carton whipping cream, whipped

- Preheat oven to 325°.

- Beat egg whites with ⅛ teaspoon salt and cream of tartar in bowl until foamy. Add sugar gradually, beating until very stiff peak holds. Fold in nuts and ½ teaspoon vanilla.

- Spread in sprayed 8 or 9-inch pie pan or into 8 individual pie pans. Build up sides to ½ inch above pan to form a meringue shell. Bake for 50 to 55 minutes. Cool.

- Melt chocolate in 3 tablespoons water in double boiler over low heat and stir constantly. Cool until thick. Add 1 teaspoon vanilla and fold into whipped cream. Pile into meringue shell. Chill for at least 2 hours before serving. Serves 8.

TIP: You can prepare this recipe 1 to 2 days ahead.

High Point, North Carolina is known as the Furniture Capital of the World. It is home to the International Home Furnishings Market held annually in April and October as well as some 125 furniture manufacturing facilities.

Mississippi Mud Pie

*The Mississippi Mud Pie and Mississippi Mud Cake both
allude to the muddy banks of the Mississippi River.
No one knows for sure which came first: pie or cake.*

4 ounces chocolate wafers
½ cup (1 stick) butter
1 quart coffee ice cream, softened
1½ cups chocolate fudge ice cream topping
Whipped topping, thawed
Sliced almonds

- Process wafers to crumbs. Melt butter in saucepan, add wafer crumbs and stir well. Press buttered wafer crumbs in bottom and sides of 9-inch pie pan and cool.

- Spread ice cream on top of wafer crust. Freeze for several hours or until firm. Spread fudge topping over top and freeze overnight. Serve with whipped topping and garnish with sliced almonds. Serves 6.

For decades, chocolate, cake and pudding have been combined in several different ways. The history of the Mississippi Mud Cake or Mississippi Mud Pie is uncertain; however, we do know that both gained national fame and spread from their Southern roots sometime after World War II. The tradition is believed to have begun in the Vicksburg or Natchez, Mississippi area because the original cake resembled the muddy banks of the Mississippi River. The layers of chocolate cake and pudding were topped with chocolate frosting that looked crusted and cracked, similar to the river banks in the hot summertime.

Chocolate Meringue Pie

2 egg yolks
2 cups milk, divided
½ cup sugar
⅓ cup self-rising flour*
2 tablespoons butter
¾ teaspoon vanilla
1 (8 inch) baked piecrust
½ cup semi-sweet chocolate chips
½ cup pecan pieces

- Combine egg yolks with ¼ cup milk in double boiler. Add sugar, flour and ¼ teaspoon salt and mix thoroughly. Add remaining milk.

- Cook over boiling water for about 6 to 7 minutes and stir constantly until thick. Cover and cook for additional 5 minutes.

- Remove from boiling water and stir in butter and vanilla. Pour into piecrust and sprinkle chocolate chips and pecans over filling.

Meringue:

2 egg whites
¼ cup sugar

- Preheat oven to 425°.

- Beat egg whites in bowl until foamy. Add sugar and beat until meringue forms stiff peaks. Spread over pie and bake for 10 minutes or until light brown. Serves 6.

TIP: *Protect piecrust from excess browning by placing 1-inch strip of foil around edges.*

*TIP: *If you don't have self-rising flour, add ½ teaspoon baking powder and ⅛ teaspoon salt to ⅓ cup all-purpose flour and mix well.*

Betty Gail's Brownie Pie

Really a special treat!

1 cup sugar
½ cup flour
2 eggs, beaten slightly
½ cup (1 stick) butter, melted
1 cup chopped pecans
1 cup chocolate chips
1 teaspoon vanilla
1 (9 inch) refrigerated piecrust
Whipped topping, thawed

- Preheat oven to 350°.

- Combine sugar and flour in bowl and add eggs. Add slightly cooled melted butter and mix well. Add pecans, chocolate chips and vanilla and pour into piecrust.

- Bake for 45 minutes and top with whipped topping. Serves 6.

Sinful Sundae Pie

You must do this ahead of time so it will freeze.

1 cup evaporated milk
1 (6 ounce) package semi-sweet chocolate pieces
1 cup miniature marshmallows
1 quart vanilla ice cream, softened
1 (9 inch) vanilla wafer crumb crust (recipe follows)
Chopped walnuts or slivered almonds, toasted

• Combine evaporated milk, chocolate and ¼ teaspoon salt in saucepan. Stir over low heat until mixture melts and is thick. Remove from heat and add marshmallows. Stir until they melt and are smooth. Cool to room temperature.

• Spoon half ice cream into crust. Cover with half chocolate mixture. Repeat layers. Garnish with nuts and freeze until firm, at least 5 hours.

Vanilla Wafer Crumb Crust:

1½ cups vanilla wafer crumbs
¼ cup (½ stick butter, softened

• Preheat oven to 350°.

• Combine ingredients until they blend well and press into 9-inch pie pan. Bake for 10 minutes. Cool. Serves 8.

Edna Mae's Chocolate Pie

¾ cup sugar
3 tablespoons flour
¼ cup (½ stick) butter
3 egg yolks, beaten
1 (12 ounce) can evaporated milk
5.5 ounces chocolate syrup
1 tablespoon vanilla
1 (9 inch) baked piecrust
Whipped cream or whipped topping, thawed

- Mix sugar and flour in saucepan. Add butter, ¼ teaspoon
  salt, egg yolks, evaporated milk, chocolate syrup and vanilla.
  Stir until all ingredients are moist.

- Bring to a boil and cook for 8 to 10 minutes. Stir constantly.
  Cool and stir several times. Pour into piecrust. Top with
  whipped cream or whipped topping. Garnish with shaved
  chocolate, if desired. Serves 8.

*Great Smoky Mountains National Park in
Tennessee and North Carolina was named for the
smoke-like blue haze often enveloping the mountains.
It is the most visited national park in the United
States.*

German Chocolate Pie

This is so easy and you can make it ahead of time and freeze.

3 cups sugar
7 tablespoons cocoa
4 eggs, beaten
1 teaspoon vanilla
1 (12 ounce) can evaporated milk
½ cup (1 stick) butter, melted
2 cups flaked coconut
1 cup chopped nuts
2 (9 inch) refrigerated piecrusts

- Preheat oven to 350°.

- Combine sugar, pinch of salt and cocoa in bowl. Add eggs and mix well. Stir in vanilla and evaporated milk. Add butter, coconut and nuts.

- Pour into piecrusts. Bake for 40 minutes or until firm. Serves 12.

The New Madrid earthquakes occurred between December 16, 1811, and February 7, 1812, in northwestern Tennessee and surrounding areas including parts of Missouri, Arkansas, Mississippi, Kentucky, Illinois and Indiana. Church bells were caused to ring as far away as Boston, Massachusetts, and the series of quakes had a greater effect on the topography of North America than any other in history. Three are thought to have exceeded 8.0 magnitude on the Richter scale. Reelfoot Lake in Obion and Lake Counties in Tennessee was formed as a result of the earthquakes.

Peach Fried Pies

Filling:

1 (8 ounce) package dried peaches
1 cup sugar

- Rinse peaches and place in large pot. Barely cover with cold water; cover and simmer over low heat until tender. Mash peaches, add sugar and blend well. Cool completely.

Crust:

1 cup shortening
4 cups flour
Vegetable oil or shortening for frying
Powdered sugar

- Cut shortening into flour and ½ teaspoon salt in bowl until crumbly. Gradually add 1 cup ice water and work together using fingers. Roll out on floured board to ⅛ inch thickness. Cut in 3½-inch circles and roll each circle again slightly for thinner edge.

- Place 1 heaping teaspoon of filling in each circle. Fold circle in half (use ice water to help seal edges together).

- With ⅓ inch melted shortening or vegetable oil in large skillet, fry both sides of pies until golden brown. Remove to paper towels and drain. Sprinkle powdered sugar over top while hot. Serves 8 to 10.

TIP: Substitute dried apples or dried apricots for peaches.

Quick and Easy Peach Cobbler

1 (20 ounce) can peach pie filling
1 (20 ounce) can crushed pineapple with juice
1 cup chopped pecans
1 (18 ounce) box yellow cake mix
1 cup (2 sticks) butter, melted
Whipped topping, thawed, or ice cream

- Preheat oven to 375°.

- Pour pie filling into sprayed 9 x 13-inch baking dish and spread evenly.

- Spoon pineapple and juice over pie filling. Sprinkle pecans over pineapple and then sprinkle cake mix over pecans. Drizzle melted butter over cake mix. Do NOT stir.

- Bake for 40 minutes or until light brown and crunchy. Serve hot or at room temperature with whipped topping or ice cream. Serves 16 to 18.

TIP: For variety, substitute apricot or cherry pie filling for peach.

Peaches are a great source of vitamin C and fiber. One peach provides 10% of the daily requirement of vitamin C and 8% of the daily requirement of fiber.

Date-Pecan Tarts

1 (8 ounce) package chopped dates
2½ cups milk
½ cup flour
1½ cups sugar
3 eggs, beaten
1 teaspoon vanilla
1 cup chopped pecans
8 tart shells, baked, cooled
1 (8 ounce) carton whipping cream
3 tablespoons powdered sugar

- Cook dates, milk, flour and sugar in saucepan until thick and stir constantly. Add eggs and ½ teaspoon salt. Cook for 5 minutes on medium heat and stir constantly.

- Stir in vanilla and pecans and pour into tart shells. Cool. Whip cream in bowl and add powdered sugar. Top each tart with a heaping tablespoon whipped cream. Serves 8.

Shelled pecans may be stored in the refrigerator for a maximum of 9 months. If stored in sealed freezer bags, pecans may keep for up to 2 years. Unshelled pecans may be stored in an airtight container in a dry, cool place for up to 6 months.

Mincemeat

This is the real deal!

3 pounds lean beef (round steak), boiled
1 pound suet
2 pounds raisins, seeded or seedless
½ pound citron
Juice and grated peel of 1½ lemons
Juice and grated peel of 1½ oranges
½ peck (6 pounds) apples
2 cups sugar
2¼ cups packed brown sugar
1¼ quarts apple cider
1 teaspoon ground ginger
2 teaspoons ground cinnamon
1 teaspoon ground cloves
2 teaspoons ground allspice
1 teaspoon ground nutmeg
½ - 1 cup sherry

- Grind cooked lean beef, suet, raisins and citron. Place in large pan or tub. Add lemon and orange juices and peels. Clean grinder; then grind peeled, cored apples and add to mixture.

- Add sugar, brown sugar, cider, ginger, cinnamon, cloves, allspice, nutmeg, and ½ teaspoon each of salt and pepper and mix well. Add sherry. Cover and place in cool (50°) place to "age". Allow at least 2 weeks to age. Check temperature daily and add sherry to suit your own taste.

- When aging is complete, package in quart containers in refrigerator or freezer until ready to make into pies. Begin shortly after Thanksgiving and your mincemeat will be ready in time for Christmas pies. Yields 3 quarts.

Favorite Chocolate Chip Cookies

½ cup (1 stick) butter, softened
¾ cup sugar
¾ cup packed brown sugar
1 egg
½ teaspoon vanilla
1 cup flour
½ teaspoon baking soda
1½ cups quick-cooking oats
1 (6 ounce) package chocolate chips
½ cup chopped pecans

• Preheat oven to 350°.

• Combine butter, sugar, brown sugar, egg, 1 tablespoon water and vanilla in bowl and beat well. Add flour and baking soda and mix well.

• Add oats, chocolate chips and pecans and mix well. Drop teaspoonfuls of mixture onto cookie sheet and bake for 12 to 15 minutes or until light brown. Yields 3 to 4 dozen.

Pecan Drops

*This is another of the easy cookie
recipes you can whip up in a jiffy.*

½ cup (1 stick) butter, softened
½ cup plus 2 tablespoons shortening
1 cup powdered sugar
2½ cups cake flour
2 teaspoons vanilla
1 cup chopped pecans

- Preheat oven to 325°.

- Cream butter and shortening in bowl until smooth. Beat in powdered sugar gradually. Stir in flour thoroughly and add vanilla and pecans.

- Drop teaspoonfuls of mixture onto cookie sheet. Bake for 15 to 20 minutes or until delicate light brown. Yields 3 to 4 dozen.

Pecans are the only major tree nut native to North America. Lumberton, Mississippi is the home of the world's largest pecan nursery.

Miss Sadie: *"Honey, don't you forget to write 'thank you' notes. When someone is thoughtful enough to do something nice for you, you should be thoughtful enough to thank them properly."*

Shortbread Crunchies

1 cup (2 sticks) butter, softened
1 cup vegetable oil
1 cup sugar
1 cup packed brown sugar
1 egg
1 teaspoon vanilla
1 cup quick-cooking oats
3½ cups flour
1 teaspoon baking soda
1 cup crushed corn flakes
1 (3.5 ounce) can flaked coconut
1 cup chopped pecans

- Preheat oven to 350°.

- Cream butter, oil, sugar and brown sugar in bowl; then add egg and vanilla and mix well. Add oats, flour, baking soda and 1 teaspoon salt and mix. Add cornflakes, coconut and pecans and mix.

- Drop teaspoonfuls of mixture onto cookie sheet. Flatten with fork dipped in water and bake for 15 minutes or until only slightly brown. Yields 4 dozen.

The Mississippi River's nickname is "Old Man River" and it is the largest river in the United States as well as the nation's chief waterway. The name "Mississippi" is derived from Native American words meaning "the father of the waters" or "great river".

Christmas Cookies

1 cup (2 sticks) butter, softened
1½ cups sugar
¼ teaspoon ground nutmeg
1 teaspoon vanilla
3 eggs
1 teaspoon baking soda
2½ cups flour
1½ cups chopped pecans
1½ cups raisins
2 cups chopped dates
1 cup candied pineapple
1 cup candied cherries

- Preheat oven to 350°.

- With mixer, cream butter and sugar in bowl. Add nutmeg, vanilla, eggs, baking soda and flour and mix well.

- Combine pecans, raisins, dates, pineapple and cherries in bowl with large spoon and add to batter. Drop teaspoonfuls on sprayed cookie sheet and bake for 12 minutes or until done. Yields 3 to 4 dozen.

The world's longest explored cave is Mammoth Cave in Kentucky. It was first promoted in 1838 and is the second oldest tourist attraction in the United States. Before being promoted as a tourist destination, the cave was mined for saltpeter and calcium nitrate.

All-Kids Peanut Butter Cookies

½ cup (1 stick) butter, softened
¼ cup shortening
⅔ cup sugar
1 cup packed brown sugar
1 egg
1 cup crunchy peanut butter
1¾ cups flour
½ teaspoon baking powder
¾ teaspoon baking soda

• Preheat oven to 350°.

• Cream butter, shortening, sugar, brown sugar and egg
  in bowl and beat well. Add peanut butter and mix. Add
  flour, baking powder, baking soda and ¼ teaspoon salt and
  mix well.

• Using small cookie scoop, place cookies onto cookie sheet.
  Use fork to flatten cookies and criss-cross fork marks twice.
  Bake for 12 minutes. Store covered. Yields 2 to 3 dozen.

*Peanut butter cookies probably originated with
George Washington Carver, a scientist from Alabama's
Tuskegee Institute who developed hundreds of
uses for peanuts. In 1916 he wrote a paper listing
105 ways to prepare peanuts for human consumption
and included three recipes for peanut cookies with chopped or
crushed peanuts. With discoveries of more than 300 ways to use
peanuts, he is considered the father of the peanut industry.*

Peanut Krispies

½ cup (1 stick) butter
2 cups peanut butter
1 (1 pound) box powdered sugar
3½ cups rice crispy cereal
¾ cup chopped peanuts

- Melt butter in large saucepan. Add peanut butter and powdered sugar and mix well. Add cereal and peanuts and mix well. Drop teaspoonfuls of mixture onto wax paper. Yields 2 to 3 dozen.

Potato Chip Cookies

Freeze these if you want to eat them in several weeks.

1 cup (2 sticks) butter, softened
½ cup sugar
1¾ cups flour
1 teaspoon vanilla
½ cup finely chopped pecans
½ cup crushed potato chips
¼ cup powdered sugar

- Preheat oven to 350°.

- Cream butter, sugar, flour and vanilla in bowl and mix well. Add pecans, stir and add potato chips.

- Drop heaping tablespoons on cookie sheet. Press flat with fork. Bake for 13 minutes and sprinkle with powdered sugar. Yields 2 to 3 dozen.

Advent Spice Cookies

This recipe is easily doubled. It's so good!

¾ **cup shortening**
1 **cup packed brown sugar**
1 **egg**
¼ **cup molasses**
2¼ **cups flour**
2 **teaspoons baking soda**
½ **teaspoon ground cloves**
1 **teaspoon ground cinnamon**
1 **teaspoon ground ginger**
Sugar

- Preheat oven to 375°.

- Thoroughly mix shortening, brown sugar, egg and molasses in bowl.

- In separate bowl, sift flour, baking soda, cloves, cinnamon, ginger and ¼ teaspoon salt and stir into first mixture.

- Chill dough and shape into large marble-size balls. Roll in sugar and place balls about 2 inches apart on sprayed cookie sheet.

- Bake for 10 to 12 minutes. Cool for 2 minutes on cookie sheet. Yields 2 to 3 dozen.

In 1983, Arkansas became the first state to require teachers to pass a basic skills test.

Orange Balls

There's nothing hard about these delicious
cookies and they will keep for several weeks.

1 (12 ounce) box vanilla wafers, crushed
½ cup orange juice concentrate, thawed
1 cup powdered sugar, divided
¾ cup shredded coconut
½ cup chopped pecans
Additional powdered sugar

• Combine vanilla wafers, orange juice, powdered sugar,
  coconut and pecans in bowl. Blend mixture well, shape into
  balls and store in covered container. Before serving, roll in
  additional powdered sugar. Yields 2 to 3 dozen.

One of the few remaining free-flowing rivers in the
lower 48 states is the Buffalo National River. It cuts
through massive limestone bluffs as it flows through
the Ozark Mountains in Arkansas.

Bourbon Balls

1 (6 ounce) package chocolate chips
½ cup sugar
3 tablespoons light corn syrup
½ cup bourbon
2½ cups finely crushed vanilla wafers
1 cup finely chopped nuts
Powdered sugar

- Melt chocolate in double boiler. Remove from heat and stir in sugar and corn syrup. Add bourbon and blend well.

- Combine vanilla wafers and nuts in large bowl. Add chocolate mixture and blend well. If mixture is too sticky, add a few more crushed vanilla wafers. Form into 1-inch balls and roll in powdered sugar. Place in airtight container for 3 days. Yields 2 to 3 dozen.

TIP: *These keep very well so they are good ones to make in advance.*

Nowhere in Kentucky is the feeling of the Old South more obvious than at My Old Kentucky Home State Park in Bardstown. Made famous by Stephen Foster's song, the home of Judge John Rowan was built in 1795 and has been preserved much as it was when Stephen Foster visited there in the 1850's.

Rum Balls

This is so easy!

½ **pound vanilla wafers**
1¼ **cups powdered sugar, divided**
2 **tablespoons cocoa**
1 **cup finely chopped pecans**
½ **cup light corn syrup**
¼ **cup rum or bourbon**

- Roll vanilla wafers into fine crumbs with rolling pin. Mix all ingredients, except ¼ cup powdered sugar in bowl, and set aside for 1 hour.

- Coat hands with remaining powdered sugar and shape mixture into 1-inch balls. Before serving, roll in powdered sugar. Yields 2 to 3 dozen.

Almond-Fudge Shortbread

1 cup (2 sticks) butter, softened
1 cup powdered sugar
1¼ cups flour
1 (12 ounce) package chocolate chips
1 (14 ounce) can sweetened condensed milk
½ teaspoon almond extract
1 (2.5 ounce) package slivered almonds, toasted

- Preheat oven to 350°.

- Beat butter, powdered sugar and ¼ teaspoon salt in bowl and stir in flour. Pat into sprayed 9 x 13-inch baking pan and bake for 15 minutes.

- Melt chocolate chips with sweetened condensed milk in medium saucepan over low heat; stir constantly until chips melt. Stir in almond extract and spread evenly over shortbread. Sprinkle with almonds.

- Chill for several hours until firm and cut into bars. These may be stored at room temperature. Yields 2 to 3 dozen.

The Kentucky Derby is one of the best-known sporting events in the U.S. and is called the "Most Exciting Two Minutes in Sports". The 1.25 mile race is for three-year-old thoroughbred horses. The race is the premier event in a 2-week schedule of parties, parades, picnics and fireworks. Meriwether Lewis Clark, grandson of the explorer William Clark of the Lewis and Clark expedition, first organized the race in 1875.

Chocolate-Caramel Bars

Truly unusual and delicious!

1 (14 ounce) bag light caramels (about 50 pieces)
1 (5 ounce) can evaporated milk, divided
1 (18 ounce) box German chocolate cake mix
¾ cup (1½ sticks) butter, melted
1 cup chopped nuts
1 cup chocolate chips

- Preheat oven to 350°.

- Melt caramels with ⅓ cup evaporated milk in double boiler.

- Combine cake mix, butter and remaining evaporated milk and mix well. Spread half cake mixture into sprayed 9 x 13-inch baking dish. Bake for 6 minutes and remove from oven.

- Sprinkle with nuts and chocolate chips and spread caramel mixture on top. Spread remainder of cake mixture and bake for 15 to 18 minutes. Remove from oven and cool before cutting into bars. Yields 18 bars.

TIP: If you use cake mix with pudding, bake for 18 to 20 minutes.

Europeans first settled in Maryland in 1631 on the Isle of Kent. Both Baltimore and Annapolis, Maryland briefly served as capitals of the U.S. In the 19th century Baltimore Harbor was home to large clipper ships built nearby.

Magic Cookie Bars

These easy bars can be assembled in baking pan for easy cleanup.

1½ cups crushed corn flake
3 tablespoons sugar
½ cup (1 stick) butter, melted
1 cup coarsely chopped walnuts or pecans
1 (6 ounce) package semi-sweet chocolate chips
1⅓ cups flaked coconut
1 (14 ounce) can sweetened condensed milk

- Preheat oven to 350°.

- Combine corn flakes, sugar, and butter in bowl and mix thoroughly. Pour mixture into 9 x 13-inch baking pan. With back of tablespoon, press mixture evenly and firmly in bottom of pan to form crust.

- Sprinkle nuts, chocolate chips and coconut evenly over crumb crust. Pour sweetened condensed milk evenly over nuts and bake for 25 minutes or until light brown around edges. Cool and cut into bars. Yields 16 to 18 bars.

Selling shoes in boxes was a concept that started in 1884 in Vicksburg, Mississippi at Phil Gilbert's Shoe Parlor on Washington Street.

Oatmeal Crispies

1 cup (2 sticks) butter, softened
1 cup sugar
1 cup packed brown sugar
2 eggs, beaten
1 teaspoon vanilla
1½ cups flour
1 teaspoon baking soda
3 cups quick-cooking oats
½ cup chopped nuts
1 teaspoon ground cinnamon

- Preheat oven to 350°.

- Cream butter, sugar and brown sugar in bowl; add eggs and vanilla and mix well.

- In separate bowl, sift flour, 1 teaspoon salt and baking soda and add to batter. Add oats, nuts and cinnamon. Shape into rolls and wrap in wax paper. Chill.

- Line cookie sheets with foil or spray cookie sheets. Slice cookies, place on cookie sheets and dip in extra sugar for a different taste. Bake for 8 to 12 minutes. Yields 18 to 20.

TIP: These are so easy and they may be frozen. Freeze dough in rolls and slice while still frozen.

Ice Box Cookies

1 cup shortening
1 cup sugar
¼ cup packed brown sugar
1 egg
1½ teaspoons vanilla
2 cups flour
2 teaspoons baking powder
1 cup chopped pecans

- Preheat oven to 350°.

- Combine shortening, sugar, brown sugar, egg, ¼ teaspoon salt and vanilla in bowl and mix well. Add flour and baking powder and mix until it blends well. Add pecans and mix.

- Divide dough in half and roll in log shape on wax paper. Roll remaining half into another log. Chill for several hours.

- Slice into ¼-inch slices. Place on cookie sheet and bake for 15 minutes or until slightly brown. Yields 2 to 3 dozen.

More than 100 buildings in Natchez, Mississippi are listed in the National Register of Historic Places.

Blonde Brownies

These are unbelievably delicious and so easy.
They store well and you can even freeze them.

1 cup (2 sticks) butter
1 (1 pound) box light brown sugar
2 eggs
2 cups flour
2 teaspoons baking powder
1 teaspoon vanilla
1 cup chopped pecans

- Preheat oven to 350°.

- Melt butter in heavy saucepan. Add brown sugar and stir in eggs, flour and baking powder. Add vanilla, a pinch of salt and pecans.

- Pour in sprayed 9 x 13-inch baking pan. Bake for 25 minutes. Yields 16.

The Okefenokee Swamp in Georgia provides sanctuary for hundreds of bird species and wildlife including endangered species. It encompasses approximately 700 square miles and is the largest intact wilderness swamp in North America. The word "Okefenokee" is derived from the Seminoles and means "land of trembling earth".

Hello Dollies

½ cup (1 stick) butter
1 cup graham cracker crumbs
1 (3.5 ounce) package flaked coconut
1 (6 ounce) package butterscotch chips
1 (6 ounce) package chocolate chips
1 cup pecan pieces
1 (14 ounce) can sweetened condensed milk

- Preheat oven to 350°.

- Melt butter in 9 x 9-inch pan. Spread crumbs in bottom of pan over butter. Layer coconut, butterscotch chips, chocolate chips and pecans.

- Pour sweetened condensed milk over top and bake for 30 minutes. Corners will brown. Cool and cut into squares. Yields 12 squares.

Blackbeard Island, Georgia was the home of the pirate Edward "Blackbeard" Teach. It includes Blackbeard Island National Wilderness and Blackbeard Island National Wildlife Refuge. Rumors of buried treasure exist, but none has ever been found.

Miss Sadie: "Honey, the family and the home are the most important things in the world. You take good care of 'em now and go bake some cookies."

Toffee Squares

1 cup (2 sticks) plus 2 tablespoons butter, softened, divided
1 cup packed brown sugar
1 egg yolk, beaten
1 teaspoon vanilla
2 cups flour
1 (8 ounce) chocolate bar
1 cup chopped nuts

- Preheat oven to 350°.

- Cream 1 cup butter and brown sugar in bowl until light. Add egg yolk, vanilla and flour.

- Spread dough thin on cookie sheet and bake for 15 to 20 minutes. Cool slightly.

- Melt chocolate with 2 tablespoons butter in double boiler and spread on cookie surface. Sprinkle with nuts and cut into squares. Yields 10 to 12.

Ellie's Easy Apple Crisp

You will love making this quick and easy dessert.

2 (20 ounce) cans apple pie filling
Lemon juice
Ground cinnamon
1 (18 ounce) box yellow cake mix
1 cup chopped walnuts
1 cup (2 sticks) butter, melted
Ice cream or whipped cream

• Preheat oven to 350°.

• Pour apple pie filling into sprayed 9 x 13-inch baking pan and squeeze small amount of lemon juice over apples. Sprinkle generously with cinnamon.

• Add cake mix over apples and sprinkle with more cinnamon. Spread walnuts on top and pour melted butter over entire mixture. Bake for 1 hour. Serve hot, plain or with ice cream or whipped cream. Serves 16 to 18.

Mildred and Patty Hill from Louisville, Kentucky created the song, "Happy Birthday to You", in 1893.

Cherry Crunch

1 (20 ounce) can cherry pie filling
1 (20 ounce) can crushed pineapple with juice
1 (18 ounce) box yellow cake mix
1 cup (2 sticks) butter, melted
½ cup chopped pecans

- Preheat oven to 350°.

- Combine pie filling and pineapple in bowl and mix well. Pour in sprayed 9 x 13-inch baking dish and sprinkle dry cake mix over mixture.

- Pour butter evenly over cake. Bake for 30 minutes, remove from oven and sprinkle pecans over top. Return to oven for additional 30 minutes.

- Let stand at room temperature for at least 20 minutes before serving. Serves 16 to 18.

In 1912, West Virginia became the first state to officially recognize Mother's Day. It became a national observance in 1914.

Curried Fruit

Delicious with ham, lamb or poultry!

1 (16 ounce) can peach halves
1 (20 ounce) can pineapple slices
1 (16 ounce) can pear halves
5 maraschino cherries
⅓ cup (⅔ stick) butter
¾ cup packed light brown sugar
2 - 4 teaspoons curry powder

- Preheat oven to 325°.

- Drain fruit and dry on paper towels. Arrange fruit in 1½-quart baking dish. Melt butter in saucepan, add brown sugar and curry powder. Spoon mixture over fruit.

- Bake for 1 hour and chill. Reheat at 350° for 30 minutes before serving. Serves 12.

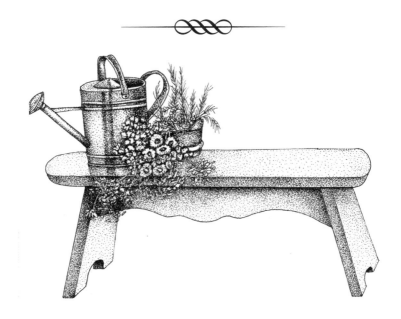

Hot Fruit Casserole

1 (16 ounce) can peaches
1 (16 ounce) can pineapple chunks
1 (16 ounce) can pear halves
1 (14 ounce) jar apple rings
2 tablespoons cornstarch
½ cup packed brown sugar
½ cup sherry
¼ cup (½ stick) butter

- Preheat oven to 350°.

- Drain fruit and save juice from peaches, pineapple and apple rings to make 2 cups liquid in bowl; set aside fruit. Add cornstarch, brown sugar, sherry and butter to juice and cook until thick.

- Arrange fruit attractively in long baking dish. Pour thickened sauce over casserole and bake for 20 minutes. Serve with any meat. Serves 12.

The first attempt to colonize America by English-speaking people was in coastal North Carolina. Two colonies were started in the 1580's under a charter granted by Queen Elizabeth to Sir Walter Raleigh. The first colony was established under the leadership of Ralph Lane in 1585 but ended in failure. The second was established on Roanoke Island in 1587 where the first child of English ancestry in the American colonies, Virginia Dare, was born. This colony vanished and the mystery of its disappearance remains today.

Weezie's Peach Crisp

You will love this easy peachy dish.

1½ quarts peaches, peeled, sliced
1½ cups sugar, divided
Lemon juice
Ground nutmeg
Ground cinnamon
½ cup (1 stick) butter, melted
¾ cup self-rising flour
Whipped cream or ice cream

- Preheat oven to 350°.

- Arrange peaches and ½ cup sugar in 3-quart baking dish. Sprinkle lemon juice, nutmeg and cinnamon as desired.

- Mix butter, flour and remaining sugar in bowl and spread topping over peaches. Bake for 30 to 35 minutes or until brown. Serve plain or with whipped cream or ice cream. Serves 8 to 10.

TIP: *Apples may be substituted for peaches.*

TIP: *If you don't have self-rising flour, add 1½ teaspoons baking powder and ½ teaspoon salt to 1 cup all-purpose flour and mix well.*

1 pound fresh peaches = 3 medium peaches = 2 cups sliced = 1½ cups peach puree.

Orange-Spiced Peaches

1 (28 ounce) can peach halves with juice
1 teaspoon whole cloves
6 sticks cinnamon
10 whole allspice
½ cup vinegar
⅔ cup sugar
1 orange, sliced

- Drain peaches and set aside ½ cup syrup. Tie cloves, cinnamon and allspice in small piece of cheesecloth.

- Combine vinegar, sugar and orange slices in large saucepan. Add drained peach halves, set aside peach syrup and spice bag. Heat to a boil, reduce heat and simmer for 5 minutes.

- Cover and let cool to room temperature. Remove spice bag and serve peach halves with orange slices. Serve warm or cold. Serves 8.

Samuel H. Rumph created the Elberta peach in 1870 in Marshallville, Georgia. He named the peach in honor of his wife. Big, beautiful and delicious, the Elberta peach was for many years the most widely raised peach in the world.

Peach Sauce

6 cups fresh peaches, peeled, sliced
¾ cup sugar
¼ teaspoon ground cinnamon
Pound cake or ice cream

- Combine peaches and 1 cup water in large saucepan and cook over medium heat for 10 minutes. Reduce heat, cover and simmer for additional 10 minutes. Cool.

- Combine peaches, sugar and cinnamon in blender and process until smooth and creamy. Pour mixture into pint jars and chill. Serve over pound cake or ice cream. Yields 2 pints.

Charlotte Russe

1 tablespoon unflavored gelatin
½ cup milk, warm
1 (8 ounce) carton whipping cream
¼ cup sugar
½ jigger (1½ tablespoons) brandy
Ladyfingers or pound cake

- Dissolve gelatin in warm milk in bowl and cool slightly.

- In separate bowl, whip cream and add sugar and brandy. Fold whipped cream mixture into gelatin mixture and pour into dish lined with ladyfingers or thinly sliced pound cake. Chill for 3 to 4 hours or until well set. Serves 6 to 8.

Chocolate Leaves

4 ounces semi-sweet chocolate pieces
Non-poisonous leaves with well-defined veins and
at least ¼-inch stems

- Melt chocolate. Wash leaves and dry. Brush melted chocolate on underside of leaves with clean ½-inch artist's brush. Put in freezer for 2 to 3 minutes or until hard enough to peel leaf from chocolate.

- Place chocolate leaves in plastic bag with air in it to cushion leaves. Keep chilled until needed.

- To keep leaves for longer time, use 6 ounces melted semi-sweet chocolate combined with block of melted paraffin and follow preceding directions.

TIP: A camellia leaf is a good choice because of its size. Rose, lemon, orange, bay, ficus and holly leaves are also good.

Traditional Custard

1 tablespoon flour
1 cup sugar
5 whole eggs
1 gallon milk
1 teaspoon vanilla

- Combine flour and sugar in bowl and stir.

- In separate bowl, beat eggs well and add milk. Combine with flour-sugar mixture and stir until sugar dissolves.

- Pour mixture into double boiler, stir constantly and cook until thick. Remove from heat, stir in vanilla and pour into custard cups. Serves 8.

Mother's Boiled Custard

½ cup sugar
4 eggs, slightly beaten
1 gallon milk
2 teaspoons vanilla

- Combine sugar, dash of salt and eggs in bowl and mix well.

- Scald milk in double boiler and add a little into egg mixture. Stir egg mixture into remaining milk in double boiler and cook. Stir constantly until mixture is thick enough to coat spoon. Remove from heat and add vanilla. Chill until ready to serve. Serves 8.

TIP: *Serve custard in glass bowls with dollop of whipped topping over top.*

Creamy Banana Pudding

1 (14 ounce) can sweetened condensed milk
1 (3.5 ounce) package instant vanilla pudding mix
1 (8 ounce) carton whipped topping, thawed
36 vanilla wafers
3 bananas, sliced

- Combine sweetened condensed milk and 1½ cups cold water in bowl. Add pudding mix and beat well. Chill for 5 minutes and fold in whipped topping. Spoon 1 cup pudding mixture into 3-quart glass serving bowl.

- Top with one-third vanilla wafers, one-third bananas and one-third remaining pudding. Repeat layers twice, ending with pudding. Cover and keep chilled. Serves 8 to 10.

Bread Pudding with Whiskey Sauce

3 tablespoons butter
1 loaf French bread
1 quart milk
3 eggs
2 cups sugar
2 tablespoons vanilla
1 cup raisins

- Preheat oven to 350°.

- Melt butter in 3-quart baking dish and cool. Soak bread in milk in bowl and crush with hands. Mix thoroughly. Add eggs, sugar, vanilla and raisins and stir well. Pour mixture over melted butter and bake 55 to 60 minutes or until very firm.

- Cool, cube pudding and pour into individual dessert dishes. When ready to serve, add Whiskey Sauce (recipe below).

Whiskey Sauce:

1 cup sugar
½ cup (1 stick) butter
1 egg, well beaten
Whiskey

- Heat sugar and butter in double boiler until sugar completely dissolves. Add egg, beating quickly so egg doesn't curdle. Cool and add whiskey to taste. Serves 8.

Pecan Bread Pudding with Bourbon Sauce

3 eggs
1½ cups sugar
2 tablespoons brown sugar
½ teaspoon ground nutmeg
2¾ cups whipping cream
¼ cup (½ stick) butter, melted
½ cup pecans
½ cup raisins
4 cups Texas toast (thickly sliced bread), crust
    removed, cubed

- Preheat oven to 375°.

- Combine 3 eggs, sugar, brown sugar, nutmeg, whipping cream, butter, pecans and raisins in bowl. Place bread in 6 x 10-inch loaf pan and pour mixture over bread. Cover and bake for 20 minutes. Uncover, bake for additional 30 minutes and cool.

Bourbon Sauce:

½ cup sugar
3 tablespoons brown sugar
1 tablespoon flour
1 egg
2 tablespoons butter, melted
1¼ cups whipping cream
¼ cup bourbon

- Whisk sugar, brown sugar, flour, egg, butter and whipping cream in heavy pan. Cook over medium heat and stir constantly until mixture is thick. Add bourbon to sauce and mix well. Slice bread pudding and serve with 2 to 3 tablespoons bourbon sauce. Serves 8.

Old-Fashioned Rice Pudding

1 cup rice
1 quart milk
½ cup (1 stick) butter
5 eggs
¾ cup sugar
½ cup raisins
1 teaspoon vanilla
2 teaspoons ground cinnamon

- Preheat oven to 350°.

- Combine rice, milk and butter in saucepan. Bring to a boil; cover and cook over low heat until rice is tender and absorbs most of milk.

- Add eggs, sugar, raisins and vanilla to mixture and pour into sprayed 2-quart baking dish. Sprinkle cinnamon on top and bake for 25 minutes. Serves 8.

Sweet Potato Pudding

2 cups grated sweet potato
¾ cup packed brown sugar
2 small eggs, beaten
¼ teaspoon ground cloves
¼ teaspoon ground allspice
½ teaspoon ground cinnamon
½ cup milk
⅓ cup orange juice
⅓ cup (⅔ stick) butter, melted

- Preheat oven to 350°.

- Combine all ingredients in bowl and mix well. Pour into sprayed baking dish and bake for 1 hour. Serves 8.

Buttermilk Ice Cream

1 quart buttermilk*
1 pint whipping cream
1 teaspoon vanilla
1 cup sugar

- Combine buttermilk, whipping cream, vanilla, ¼ teaspoon salt and sugar in bowl and stir until sugar dissolves. Pour into ice trays and freeze. When cream is partially frozen, remove from freezer and beat. Return to trays and freeze. Serves 6.

*TIP: To make 1 quart buttermilk, mix 1 quart milk with ¼ cup lemon juice or vinegar and let milk stand for about 10 minutes.

Homemade Peach Ice Cream

1½ quarts mashed, ripe peaches
2 tablespoons vanilla
2 (14 ounce) cans sweetened condensed milk
1 (12 ounce) can evaporated milk
½ cup sugar
½ gallon milk

- Combine peaches, vanilla, ½ teaspoon salt, sweetened condensed milk, evaporated milk and sugar in ice cream freezer container and mix well. Add milk to mixture line in container.

- Freeze according to manufacturer's directions. Serves 10 to 12.

Old-Time Peach Ice Cream

12 peaches, peeled, quartered
3 cups sugar, divided
Juice of ½ lemon
4 eggs
3 tablespoons flour
5 cups milk
1 (1 pint) carton whipping cream

- Place peaches in blender and blend with 1 cup sugar and lemon juice. Chill.

- Beat eggs slightly in bowl and add remaining sugar, flour and a pinch of salt. Place mixture in double boiler.

- Scald milk in saucepan and slowly add to egg mixture. Cook over medium heat in double boiler until thick, stirring frequently. Cool.

- Place peaches, custard and whipping cream in ice cream freezer container and stir to blend ingredients. Freeze according to manufacturer's directions. Serves 10 to 12.

Baked Caramel Corn

1 cup (2 sticks) butter
2 cups packed brown sugar
½ cup light or dark corn syrup
½ teaspoon baking soda
1 tablespoon vanilla
6 quarts popped corn

- Preheat oven to 250°.

- Melt butter in saucepan and stir in brown sugar, corn syrup and 1 tablespoon salt. Stir constantly and bring to a boil. Boil but do not stir for 5 minutes. Remove from heat and stir in baking soda and vanilla. Pour mixture over popped corn and mix well.

- Turn into 2 large shallow baking pans and bake for 1 hour. Stir every 15 minutes. Remove from oven and cool completely. Break apart and store in sealed containers. Serves 8.

The Jubilee Singers of Fisk University in Nashville introduced the beauty and tradition of the Negro spiritual to a wide audience. This became the basis for other genres of African-American music. Their successful tours to raise funds for the university during the 1870's set the stage for Nashville becoming known for music.

Creamy Pralines

2¼ cups sugar
1 (3 ounce) can evaporated milk
½ cup white corn syrup
¼ teaspoon baking soda
¼ cup (½ stick) butter
1 teaspoon vanilla
2 cups pecans

- Combine sugar, evaporated milk, corn syrup and baking soda in double boiler. Cook and stir constantly until it reaches soft-ball stage (234° to 243°) on candy thermometer. This will take about 15 minutes.

- Remove from heat and add butter, vanilla and pecans. Beat mixture until cool and stiff enough to keep its shape when dropped on wax paper. Yields 14 to 16.

Pralines

1 (1 pound) box light brown sugar
¾ cup evaporated milk
1½ cups pecan pieces or halves
1½ teaspoons instant or freeze-dried coffee granules

- Mix all ingredients thoroughly in medium saucepan, cook slowly over low heat and stir constantly until mixture reaches soft-ball stage (234° to 243°). Remove from heat and set aside for 5 minutes.

- Beat with spoon until mixture is thick. Drop teaspoonful of mixture onto sprayed foil. When cool and hard, peel foil from back and wrap each praline in plastic wrap. Yields 14 to 16.

Peanut Brittle

2 cups sugar
1 cup light corn syrup
2 cups raw peanuts
1 teaspoon vanilla
1 tablespoon baking soda

- Combine sugar, corn syrup, ½ cup water, peanuts and
  1 teaspoon salt in heavy saucepan. Boil until candy
  thermometer reaches 293°. Cool until syrup spins a thread
  (approximately 230°). Add vanilla and beat.

- Sprinkle baking soda from spoon and quickly beat well. It
  will foam. Immediately pour onto sprayed marble slab, large
  cookie sheet or large aluminum serving tray. When cool,
  break apart and store. Yields 14 to 16.

*French settlers brought pralines to Louisiana.
Originally made with almonds in France, pralines
were soon made with the locally abundant pecans.
So popular was the confection that it quickly spread
wherever pecans were plentiful. Pralines became a
traditional southern favorite.*

Easy, No-Fail Divinity

2½ cups sugar
½ cup light corn syrup
2 egg whites, stiffly beaten
1 teaspoon vanilla
¾ cup chopped pecans

• Combine sugar, corn syrup, ½ cup water and ⅛ teaspoon salt in saucepan. Boil mixture for about 4 minutes or until soft-ball stage (234° to 243°) on candy thermometer).

• Beat egg whites in bowl until fairly stiff with mixer and slowly pour half syrup into beaten whites. Beat constantly.

• Continue cooking remaining syrup until it reaches soft-crack stage (270° on candy thermometer). While still beating egg white mixture on high, slowly pour in remaining syrup. Reduce mixer speed to low and continue beating for additional 5 minutes or until teaspoon of candy stands up.

• Quickly stir in vanilla and nuts. Drop tablespoonfuls on sprayed baking sheet. Serves 14 to 16.

TIP: Soft-ball stage can be determined by dropping a drop of syrup in a cup of cold water (usually 234° on a candy thermometer). It will form a small ball.

When Georgia became a colony, every man, woman and child was promised 64 quarts of molasses if they stayed one year. Molasses was the sweetener of choice until after World War I when sugar became more affordable.

Old-Time Pull Taffy

2 cups sugar
½ cup light corn syrup
¼ teaspoon cream of tartar
½ teaspoon almond extract
Food coloring

- Combine sugar, corn syrup, ½ cup water and cream of tartar in saucepan. Heat and stir until sugar dissolves. Cook (DO NOT STIR) to 265° on candy thermometer.

- Remove from heat and stir in almond extract and coloring. Pour mixture onto sprayed platter and cool. With greased hands, pull into ropes until chalky and porous. Break or cut into bite-size pieces with scissors. Serves 14 to 16.

Family Favorite Fudge

4½ cups sugar
1 (12 ounce) can evaporated milk
1 cup (2 sticks) butter
3 (6 ounce) packages chocolate chips
1 tablespoon vanilla
1½ cups chopped pecans

- In saucepan, bring sugar and evaporated milk to a rolling boil that cannot be stirred down. Boil for exactly 6 minutes and stir constantly.

- Remove from heat, add butter and chocolate chips and stir until butter and chips melt. Add vanilla and pecans and stir well.

- Pour into sprayed 9 x 13-inch dish and set aside for at least 6 hours or overnight before cutting. Store in airtight container. Serves 12.

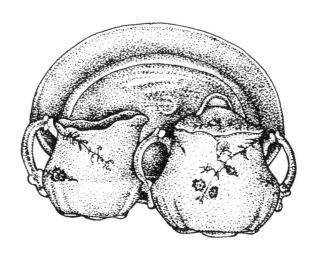

Bibliography

Classical Southern Cooking: A Celebration of the Cuisine of the Old South. Damon Lee Fowler. Gibbs Smith. Layton, Utah. 2008.

Cooking History/Traditions Archive. www.ochef.com/cooking_history.htm

History and Recipe of Collard Greens. http://whatscookingamerica.net

History of Iced Tea and Sweet Tea. http://www.whatscookingamerica. net/History/IcedTeaHistory.htm.

History of Southern Cooking and Recipes. www. ashlandbelle.com

Miss Sadie's Southern Cooking. Cookbook Resources, LLC, Highland Village, Texas. 2005.

On Southern Cooking. http://bama.ua.edu/~bgray/recipes.htm

Origin of Southern Food. http://uwf.edu

Savannah Style. Junior League of Savannah, Inc., Savannah, Georgia. 1980.

Soul Food: Classic Cuisine from the Deep South. Sheila Ferguson. Grove Press. New York, New York. 1989.

Southern Food: At Home, on the Road, in History. John Egerton, Ann Bleidt Egerton. Alfred A. Knopf, Inc. 1947. University of North Caroline Press. 1993.

The Catfish Institute. Jackson, Mississippi. www.catfishinstitute.com

The Glory of Southern Cooking. James Villas. John Wiley & Sons, Hoboken, New Jersey, 2007.

The Heritage of Southern Cooking: An Inspired Tour of Southern Cuisine Including Regional Specialties, Heirloom Favorites and Original Dishes. Camille Glenn. Black Dog Leventhal, New York, New York, 2007

Vidalia Onions, Vidalia, Georgia. www.vidalias.com

Index

G

H

I

Mississippi Mud Pie   224
Peach Cobbler, Quick and
    Easy   231
Peach Fried Pies   230
Peach Mousse Pie   210
Peach Parfait Pie   211
Peanut Pie   217
Pineapple-Coconut Pie   212
Quick and Easy Peach
    Cobbler   231
Sinful Sundae Pie   227
Sissy's Cream Puff Pie   209
Southern Whiskey Pie   219
Strawberry Pie   213
Sunny Lemon Chess Pie   221
Weezie's Peach Crisp   256
Willa Mae's Pecan Pie   218
Pimiento Cheese, Southern   15
Pineapple-Coconut Pie   212
Pirate Stew   29
Poppy Seed Cake   203
Poppy Seed Chicken   126
Pork
    Barbecued Pork Chops   146
    Barbecued Pork Roast   150
    Carolina Country Ham   156
    Carolina Pulled Pork   149
    Chicken Elegant   130
    Frogmore Stew   32
    Ginger Baby Back Ribs   151
    Grilled Pork Loin   148
    Ham and Fresh Okra Soup   24
    Hoppin' John   93
    Low Country Boil   152
    Old-Fashioned Country Ham   157
    Pan-Fried Pork Chops   144
    Pork Chop Casserole   145
    Pork Chops and Red Cabbage   143
    Pork Loin with Apricot Glaze   147
    Raisin Sauce for Ham   159
    Saucy Ham Loaf   158
    Sausage Soufflé   153
    Savory Sausage and Sweet
        Potatoes   152
    Sister's Brunswick Stew   31
    Slow-Cook Navy Bean and Ham
        Soup   25
    Smithfield Virginia Country
        Ham   154

Supreme Ham Casserole   159
Pork Chop Casserole   145
Pork Chops and Red Cabbage   143
Pork Loin with Apricot Glaze   147
Potato Chip Cookies   239
Potatoes
    Brandied Sweet Potatoes   98
    Low Country Boil   152
    Perfect Potato Salad   38
    Savory Sausage and Sweet
        Potatoes   152
    Sweet Potato Balls   97
    Sweet Potato Pudding   263
    Sweet Potato Soufflé   96
    Twice-Baked Potatoes   95
Poultry – See Chicken
Pound Cake, The Only Great   205
Praline Cheesecake   208
Pralines   267
Preserves
    Bread-and-Butter Pickles   64
    Chow-Chow   68
    Green Tomato Pickles   66
    Okra Pickles   65
    Southern Mint Jelly   63
    Watermelon Preserves   67
Puddings
    Bread Pudding with Whiskey
        Sauce   261
    Charlotte Russe   258
    Creamy Banana Pudding   260
    Mother's Boiled Custard   260
    Old-Fashioned Rice Pudding   263
    Pecan Bread Pudding with Bourbon
        Sauce   262
    Sweet Potato Pudding   263
    Traditional Custard   259
Pumpkin
    Company Pumpkin Pie   214
    Fannie's Pumpkin Cream Pie   215
    Pumpkin Bread   55
Pumpkin Bread   55
Pumpkin Cream Pie, Fannie's   215

Quail, Southern Style, Smothered   184
Quick and Easy Peach Cobbler   231

Cookbooks Published by Cookbook Resources, LLC
Bringing Family and Friends to the Table

The Best 1001 Short, Easy Recipes

1001 Slow Cooker Recipes

1001 Short, Easy, Inexpensive Recipes

1001 Fast Easy Recipes

1001 America's Favorite Recipes

Easy Slow Cooker Cookbook

Busy Woman's Slow Cooker Recipes

Busy Woman's Quick & Easy Recipes

365 Easy Soups and Stews

365 Easy Chicken Recipes

365 Easy One-Dish Recipes

365 Easy Soup Recipes

365 Easy Vegetarian Recipes

365 Easy Casserole Recipes

365 Easy Pasta Recipes

365 Easy Slow Cooker Recipes

Super Simple Cupcake Recipes

Leaving Home Cookbook and Survival Guide

Essential 3-4-5 Ingredient Recipes

Ultimate 4 Ingredient Cookbook

Easy Cooking with 5 Ingredients

The Best of Cooking with 3 Ingredients

Easy Diabetic Recipes

Ultimate 4 Ingredient Diabetic Cookbook

4-Ingredient Recipes for 30-Minute Meals

Cooking with Beer

The Washington Cookbook

The Pennsylvania Cookbook

The California Cookbook

Best-Loved New England Recipes

Best-Loved Canadian Recipes

Best-Loved Recipes from the Pacific Northwest

Easy Homemade Preserves (Handbook with Photos)

Garden Fresh Recipes (Handbook with Photos)

Easy Slow Cooker Recipes (Handbook with Photos)

Cool Smoothies (Handbook with Photos)
Easy Cupcake Recipes (Handbook with Photos)
Easy Soup Recipes (Handbook with Photos)
Classic Tex-Mex and Texas Cooking
Best-Loved Southern Recipes
Classic Southwest Cooking
Miss Sadie's Southern Cooking
Classic Pennsylvania Dutch Cooking
The Quilters' Cookbook
Healthy Cooking with 4 Ingredients
Trophy Hunter's Wild Game Cookbook
Recipe Keeper
Simple Old-Fashioned Baking
Quick Fixes with Cake Mixes
Kitchen Keepsakes & More Kitchen Keepsakes
Cookbook 25 Years
Texas Longhorn Cookbook
Gifts for the Cookie Jar
All New Gifts for the Cookie Jar
The Big Bake Sale Cookbook
Easy One-Dish Meals
Easy Potluck Recipes
Easy Casseroles Cookbook
Easy Desserts
Sunday Night Suppers
Easy Church Suppers
365 Easy Meals
Gourmet Cooking with 5 Ingredients
Muffins In A Jar
A Little Taste of Texas
A Little Taste of Texas II
Ultimate Gifts for the Cookie Jar

cookbook resources LLC
www.cookbookresources.com
Toll free 866-229-2665
Your Ultimate Source for Easy Cookbooks

Enjoy the latest releases in our
American Regional Series